Vladivostok ●

JAPAN

MONGOLIA

KOREA

CHINA

Uniforms of the
Imperial Russian Army

UNIFORMS
of the
IMPERIAL
RUSSIAN ARMY

BORIS MOLLO

illustrated by
John Mollo

BLANDFORD   PRESS
POOLE   DORSET

First published in the UK in 1979
Copyright © 1979 Blandford Press Ltd
Link House, West Street,
Poole, Dorset BH15 1LL

ISBN 0 7137 0920 0

British Library Cataloguing in Publication Data

Mollo, Boris
  Uniforms of the Imperial Russian Army.
  – (Blandford colour series).
  1. Russia. Army – Uniforms
  I. Title   II. Mollo, John
  355.1′4′0947   UC485.R

Filmset in 10 on 12pt Monophoto Baskerville
by Northumberland Press Ltd, Gateshead,
Tyne and Wear

Printed by Fletcher and Son Ltd, Norwich

Contents

Preface

The student of Russian military uniforms is probably better provided for than that of any other army. Being a centralized autocratic state, decisions were taken centrally and recorded accordingly. The Tsars themselves took a close interest in uniform and it was Nicholas I who instituted the monumental work on the history of Russian uniforms, A. V. Viskovatov's *Historical Description of the Uniforms and Armaments of the Russian Army* published between 1844 and 1856 and running to thirty volumes. Thereafter there were published continuously lists of changes with detailed illustrations and descriptions. In the last years of the old regime there was in addition a series of books produced under the editorship of Colonel V. K. Schenk which summarized regimental histories, distinctions and uniforms.

The problem in a book of this nature therefore has been less what to include than what to exclude. To tell the story of Russian uniforms from 1700 to 1917 in any detail would require a much larger book running to several volumes. The aim of this book is to draw attention to the major changes in uniform and to show something of the adaptations, official and unofficial which occurred during the major wars in which the Russian army was involved. It is also necessary to draw attention to the reasons behind the changes, the personalities of the Tsars and Tsarinas, the influence of other armies and the fashions of the times all of which profoundly affected uniform design. And through all this may be discerned the spirit of 'Mother Russia' herself, resisting too much Europeanization and, particularly in times of crisis, reverting to traditional methods. The best example of this, paradoxically, occurred outside the period covered by this book when in 1941–2, the Soviet army was reeling from the armoured onslaught of the Germans and many traditional features of Tsarist uniforms were reintroduced to foster the spirit of the armed forces. I have made extensive use of Russian uniform terminology. As a general rule the English translation has only been given on the first occasion on which a Russian word has been used and not thereafter, but all the terms used are included in the Glossary.

This book has been very much a family affair. My brother John has produced an excellent set of illustrations and his advice has been invaluable at every turn. My brother Andrew has helped with the section dealing with World War I. My father Eugene who has made a lifelong study of the Imperial Russian army and who has un- rivalled knowledge of the intricacies of its uniform has been the guiding force throughout the writing of the text.

Merton Park, London, 1979   Boris Mollo

I
Peter the Great
1686–1725

Peter I

The army which Peter the Great inherited from his father, the Tsar Alexis (1645–76) was based partly on traditional Russian lines but the process of modernization had already begun and the influence of recent developments in Western European armies was already having an effect. In time of war the main bulk of troops was provided by the *dvoriani*, best translated by the English word 'Yeomen'. They were free men, provided with land by the state and freed from paying taxes but with these privileges they were obliged to serve when called upon by the Tsar, to bring a certain number of men according to the size of their estate and to horse and arm them at their own expense. The *dvoriani*'s main service was to guard Russia's borders against raids by the Tatars and for this purpose they could raise a force of over 100,000 mounted troops. They operated from a series of fortified bases from which patrols of about 100 men at a time were sent out. In addition they could be called on to serve in major wars anywhere at the Tsar's behest.

The nearest approach to a standing army were the *strelzi*, from the word *streletz* meaning literally a 'shooter' which could therefore refer to a man armed with bow and arrow or a firearm. By the middle of the seventeenth century they were largely trained in the use of

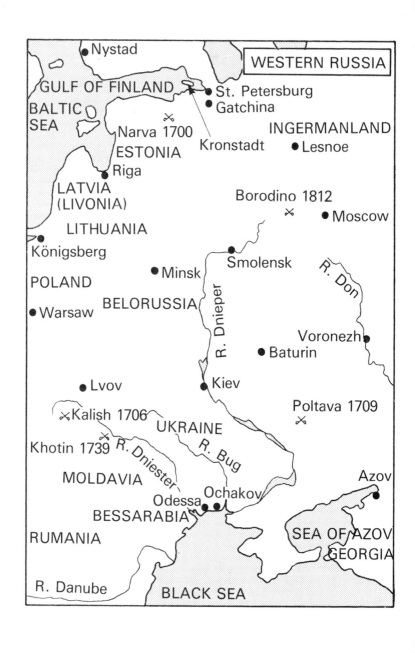

WESTERN RUSSIA

Nystad

GULF OF FINLAND

BALTIC SEA

St. Petersburg

Gatchina

Kronstadt

INGERMANLAND

Narva 1700

ESTONIA

Lesnoe

Riga

LATVIA (LIVONIA)

Borodino 1812

Moscow

LITHUANIA

Königsberg

Smolensk

R. Don

POLAND

Minsk

BELORUSSIA

R. Dnieper

Warsaw

Voronezh

Baturin

Lvov

Kiev

Poltava 1709

Kalish 1706

UKRAINE

Khotin 1739   R. Dniester

R. Bug

Azov

MOLDAVIA

Ochakov

Odessa

BESSARABIA

SEA OF AZOV

RUMANIA

GEORGIA

R. Danube

BLACK SEA

firearms. They were a caste, relatively well paid by the state, so that they were able to form their own communities or districts in a town. Here a general air of prosperity reigned, enhanced further by their custom of acting as tradesmen or craftsmen on the side. Their main task was to provide garrisons for the main towns and fortresses and they also acted as gendarmerie for the maintenance of law and order.

In larger towns they formed regiments, for example in Moscow there were fourteen regiments of *strelzi*. They selected their own junior officers from among the ranks of their caste while senior officers were selected by the Tsar from the higher nobility, the *boyars* who became known as *voyevoda* or 'leaders of troops'. Supporting the *strelzi* and organized in much the same way were the artillery or *pushkari* from *pushka* meaning a cannon. The *strelzi* were dressed in Russian style with long pointed caps of brightly coloured cloth, long *kaftans* reaching almost to the ground and yellow, red or green boots. They were armed with matchlock muskets, sabres and *berdysh* (battle-axes).

The third traditional element of armed forces at the disposal of the Tsar were the cossacks comprising mainly Russian or Don cossacks, based on the River Don, and Ukrainian cossacks based on the River Dnieper. The Don cossacks were not officially part of the Russian army but could be called out by the Tsar and were used largely for guarding the border. If required for a major campaign, they would remain under their own commanders or *ataman* and would retain their own organization. They were primarily cavalry but could also operate from river boats much as their forefathers, the Varangian Vikings who first sailed into the Gulf of Finland and thence into the great Russian river systems. Ukrainian cossacks were either in the service of the Polish crown or operated as independent bands which survived by robbing Turks or anyone else unfortunate enough to come in their way. When the Ukraine was taken over by Russia, they served the Tsar on the same basis as the Don cossacks.

In an effort to modernize the army, Tsar Alexis had formed mercenary regiments, then prevalent throughout Western Europe. Known as *innozemni* or 'foreign regiments', they were at first composed entirely of foreign mercenaries under their own officers. As time went on, Alexis commissioned mercenary officers to raise regiments of Russian nationals and these *soldatski* regiments were the forerunners of the modern Russian army. The mercenary officers, among whom were many Jacobites, brought with them up to date knowledge of

Western military science and drills and from his earliest days Peter the Great was much influenced by the Jacobite, General Patrick Gordon.

The Russian army was in this transitional state when in 1676 Tsar Alexis died. He left by his first wife Maria Miloslavskaya, two sons, Theodore and Ivan and a daughter Sophia and by his second marriage to Natalia Naryshkina, a son, Peter. The eldest son, Theodore, was proclaimed Tsar but he was already ailing and only reigned for six years. His brother Ivan was mentally retarded and an assembly called by the Patriarch proclaimed ten-year-old Peter as the new Tsar. However, at the instigation of Sophia and the Miloslavsky family, the *strelzi* insisted that Ivan should be joint Tsar and Sophia became regent. A seditious period of plots and counterplots followed. Eventually the Miloslavskys gained the upper hand and following the murder of many of the Naryshkin family and their supporters, Peter's mother retired with him to the palace of Preobrajenskoe, outside Moscow.

Here Peter grew up in relative seclusion and safety, while under the influence of General Patrick Gordon, his interest in military affairs developed. In 1683, at the age of eleven, he was allowed playmates or *poteshni* who came either from Boyar families or from the families of court servants and he formed them into a children's army of his own. Throughout his childhood, Peter's passion was his army. He was continually sending demands to the arsenal for more miniature weapons, equipment, standards and musical instruments. Eventually he outgrew Preobrajenskoe and spread into the next door property of Semenovskoe and so had the basis of what became his two senior guard regiments, the Preobrajenski and the Semenovski whose seniority dated from 1683. As his regiments approached adulthood, he persuaded General Patrick Gordon to arrange large scale exercises and he even exercised his prerogative as Tsar to call out the *strelzi* to act as enemy. Meanwhile, with the help of the Dutchman, Timmermann, he was busy learning navigation and ship-building.

Eventually Peter felt strong enough to challenge Sophia. The confrontation came in 1689 when Sophia insisted on taking part in a religious procession from which women had always been excluded. Peter ordered her to leave and when she refused, he walked out and returned to Preobrajenskoe. Shortly after his return a rumour reached him that the *strelzi* were marching towards the estate. Peter immediately took refuge in the fortified monastery of Troetsko-Sergievskaia and ordered the archimandrite to place it on a siege footing. He also called out the local *dvoriani* militia to aid in the defence and summoned two *soldatski* regiments, Gordon's and the 'Selected'. The *strelzi* meanwhile had arrived at Preobrajenskoe, found Peter gone and returned peaceably to Moscow. Sophia now became frightened. She tried to contact Peter who would not answer and sent *boyars* to negotiate but they all changed their allegiance to Peter much as Marlborough and other British generals changed their allegiance from James II to William III at almost the same time. Peter now felt strong enough to return to Moscow, oust Sophia and appoint his mother regent. A committee of *boyars* was set up to enquire into the incident and many *strelzi* were tortured and executed. Although nominally Ivan continued to share the throne until his death in 1696, Peter was now in sole charge.

Peter soon felt ready for his first campaign and he chose as his target Russia's traditional southern enemy, the Turkish Empire. His aim was to gain an outlet to the Black Sea. He formed a traditional army of *strelzi*, *dvoriani* and cossacks backed up by his two guard regiments and some *soldatski* regiments and set out to besiege Azov. He was first repulsed with heavy losses and he found that, without a navy, he could not block the water approaches to the fortress. He therefore spent the winter of 1695–6 building a fleet near Voronezh and the following spring with his own new navy and an increased military force, he finally captured Azov. The nominal head of the Azov campaign was Leforte, a mercenary officer of Swiss origin who had been a boon companion of Peter's and who was proclaimed Grand-Admiral. Peter however retained close control and relied mainly on the advice of Patrick Gordon. With the success of Azov behind him, Peter craved for more knowledge of the military and naval sciences of the west and in 1697 he set off on a grand tour of the Hanseatic ports of Germany followed by Holland and Britain.

Just over a year later, word came back that the *strelzi* had risen in rebellion. Peter hurried back to find that the revolt had been suppressed by Patrick Gordon but the *strelzi* were disbanded as an organization, many of its members were tortured and executed and others were exiled to remote garrisons. From then on garrisons were found from the ranks of elderly soldiers, while, to provide fighting troops, Peter set up and recruited a regular standing army on western lines. He was able to attract recruits by offering food, clothing, a small salary and freedom to serfs, no small incentive in seventeenth-century Russia. He kept the army simple and apart from his two guard regiments formed only *soldatski* (infantry) and *dragoonski* (mounted infantry) regiments but among other reforms he instituted forts and arsenals and founded military and naval colleges. The bulk of his army was formed in the first two or three years but he went on adding to his army in times of war and reducing it in times of peace. At his death in 1725 there were two guard regiments, fifty-one infantry and thirty-three dragoon regiments in addition to an artillery regiment, fifty garrison regiments, six regiments of Ukrainian militia, a squadron of Serbian hussars and cossacks.

Reforms were not confined to the armed forces as in all walks of life Peter insisted on westernization of dress and he banned beards. Paradoxically however he dropped the long coat or *kaftan* just as western armies were adopting it. In general the army followed western styles of uniform with each regiment having its own distinctive colour, the Preobrajenski Guard wearing green, the Semenovski, light blue and the Butyrski, the senior infantry regiment, red. At first regiments were called after their Colonels but in 1708 Peter began allocating provincial names, although this did not (and never did subsequently) imply that the soldiers of a particular regiment came from the region after which it was named. In 1704 grenadier companies were introduced and between 1708 and 1711, five grenadier regiments and three regiments of horse grenadiers were formed from existing grenadier companies. Only guard regiments retained grenadier companies and the Preobrajenski Guard also had its own regimental artillery company.

In 1700 Peter formed a secret alliance with Augustus the Strong, Elector of Saxony and King of Poland, and after negotiating peace with Turkey, he turned on Sweden and embarked on the Great Northern War which was to last from 1700 to 1721. Augustus began hostilities in June 1700 by invading Livonia and besieging Riga, followed two months later by Peter who invaded Ingermanland and laid siege to the Port of Narva. However King Charles XII of Sweden displayed his military genius by defeating the Danes and rapidly transferring his armies by sea to Narva where he surprised and defeated Peter's besieging force. The *dvoriani* fled and even the new regular regiments did not do very well, only the guard regiments standing firm for which Peter awarded their officers the privilege of wearing gorgets, a distinction retained until 1917. Peter realized that modernization must continue. The *dvoriani* militia was disbanded but its members were still obliged to serve for their estates but now in regular regiments where many became officers. Charles XII underestimating Peter's ambition and the powers of recovery of the Russian army decided to ignore Russian forces in the Baltic provinces and he turned on Augustus in Poland. Peter quietly went on with recruiting and training his new regiments and began to demonstrate signs of success, taking Narva, Nottenberg and Nienschanz which he chose as the site of his new capital, St Petersburg.

In 1706 Charles defeated Augustus in Saxony and Augustus secretly sued for peace resigning his kingship of Poland. Meanwhile a Russian corps under Menschikov had defeated a Swedish army at Kalisch in Poland and at last Charles woke up to the increasing strength and threat of Peter's new army. He turned his personal attention east and marched with his army into Poland and Western Russia. Peter now in personal command of his armies in Poland withdrew, devastating the country over which the Swedes were expected to advance. Charles, growing short of men and supplies, decided that a direct advance on Moscow was risky and since he had been promised support from Hetman Mazeppa of the Ukrainian cossacks, an army of some 60,000 men and food, artillery and a better climate, he turned south into the Ukraine. Peter and Menschikov responded by attacking Mazeppa's capital, Baturin, where they took his treasury, arsenals and reserves. A new Ataman was elected and the mass of the Ukrainian cossacks transferred their loyalty. Mazeppa with a small force fled to join Charles. Although his army was now dwindling Charles continued his advance into the Ukraine with Peter giving way before him until Charles reached and laid siege to the fortress of Poltava, which he hoped to use as a base for resting and reinforcing his army. However Loewenhaupt's Corps, his main hope for fresh troops and supplies, was trapped by a special mounted corps led by Peter himself and was defeated at the battle of Lesnaia. Peter now at last felt confident enough to attack Charles' main force at Poltava and there in June 1709 won an overwhelming victory. The Swedes fled to the Dnieper but only Charles, Mazeppa and a few bodyguards were able to cross and surrender to the Turks where Charles remained for many years. Poltava was to the Russian army what Blenheim, five years earlier, was to the British army, a victory of international proportions which placed a newly formed standing army firmly on the map.

Two years later, full of confidence after Poltava, Peter invaded the Turkish province of Moldavia but was outmanoeuvred by a larger Turkish army and was forced to sue for peace. Fortunately for Russia, the Turks allowed Peter lenient terms which involved little more than the return of Azov and other territories he had captured from them. Peter completed his conquest of the Baltic provinces and even carried the war into Finland and the mainland of Sweden until, exhausted by the war, Sweden sued for peace. By the Treaty of Nystad in 1721, Russia kept Livonia, Estonia, Ingermanland but returned most of Finland to Sweden. Russia had supplanted Sweden as the dominant power in the Baltic and now ranked as a major European power.

2
Peter's Successors
1725–1762

Elizabeth I

The thirty-seven years between the death of Peter the Great and the accession of his granddaughter-in-law, Catherine the Great, saw a gradual consolidation of Peter's efforts to westernize Russian society and her army. Thanks to the marriages of his descendants to German princes and princesses, the strongest influence came from the German states and since this was the period of the rise of Prussia as a major military force, this influence was particularly strong in military circles. Peter had encompassed the death of his only son, the Tsarevitch Alexis and so Peter's death was followed by a period of political instability during which the support of the army was essential for any aspirant to the throne and correspondingly the power of the army grew.

In 1725, the Guards headed by Feldmareshal Menschikov, proclaimed Peter's second wife, Catherine, as his successor, but she died in 1727 to be succeeded by Peter II, son of the ill-fated Alexis, who also died after a short reign. In 1739 came Anna Iovannovna, daughter of Peter's elder brother Ivan, who was married to the reigning Duke of Courland, an impoverished province of Prussia. She reigned for ten years and died nominating as her successor, her niece Anna Leopoldovna and her son Ivan. Within a year, there had been a coup

9

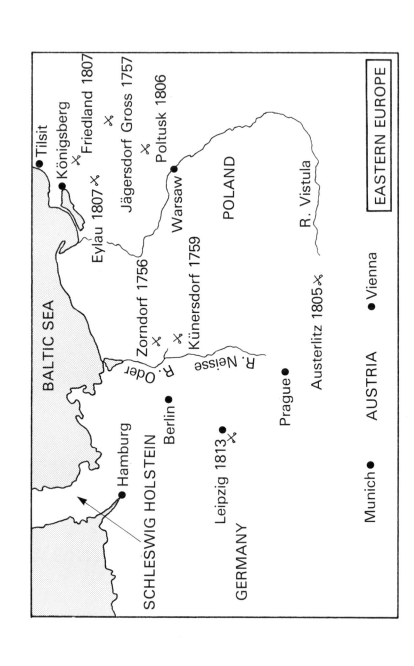

EASTERN EUROPE

d'état and with the help of the guards, the throne was taken by Elizabeth, daughter of Peter the Great and Catherine. Her reign lasted until 1762. She had brought to Russia her nephew Peter, ruling Duke of Holstein and declared him her successor. Shortly after, he married Sophia, daughter of Prince Anhalt-Zersbst, a Prussian General. Sophia adopted the Orthodox faith and the name of Catherine. Within a few months of her husband's accession, she had, again with the help of the Guard, deposed him and embarked on the long (thirty-four years) and successful reign which earned her the title of 'Catherine the Great'.

During these six reigns the army gradually developed along the lines which Peter had planned and hoped for, an essentially Russian institution which nevertheless retained contact with the west and absorbed new developments in military science. The presence of many German courtiers and soldiers meant that instructors with first hand knowledge of the techniques of the Prussian army, the most up-to-date in Europe, were always on hand.

Catherine I's reign of only three years saw no developments of any significance.

By the time Anne ascended the throne in 1730, the army was showing the effect of the absence of Peter's firm control. It was smaller, regiments were not fully recruited and the fighting edge sharpened at such cost by Peter was beginning to be blunted. Anne handed responsibility for military affairs over to Field Marshal Münnich, a German mercenary officer who had been a protégé of Peter the Great. He instituted a military commission which recommended a number of changes. The Guard was increased by two regiments, one infantry (Life-Guard Ismailovski Regiment) and one cavalry as Menschikov's Life Dragoons at last achieved full guard status as the Life-Guard Horse Regiment. It absorbed as officers any remaining members of Peter's Cavalier Guard who had only been called upon for occasional ceremonial duties. The Life-Guard Horse Regiment was equipped with cuirasses, the first time they had been used in the post-Petrovian army. The commission also recommended that ten army dragoon regiments should be converted to cuirassiers, but at first only three were, the 1st Münnich Regiment, 2nd Life Cuirassier Nevski Regiment and the 3rd Life Cuirassier Regiment. They were equipped on Prussian lines with front cuirasses only and with heavy straight broadswords or *pallasches*. The commission set the size of the Russian army at thirty-eight infantry regiments, thirty-two cavalry and forty-nine garrison regiments.

In 1730, Empress Anne confirmed the introduction of coats of arms for army units which were to appear on standards, officers' gorgets and grenadier caps. Gold and silver braid was introduced on collars and cuffs for NCOs and both officers and NCOs were given white cockades in the form of a bow.

Another recommendation of the commission had important lasting results, the formation of the 1st Cadet Corps to provide education for 200 sons of the nobility, later expanded to 360 when the nobility of the Baltic provinces were included. This was the first time that the Russian upper classes had been provided with institutionalized general education on a large scale and resulted in the growth of a military intelligentsia which played such an important part in Russia's history and which included in its ranks Tolstoy, Dostoevski, Rimsky Korsakov, Mussorgsky and many others.

Prussian influence was strong also in matters of dress and appearance. Already under Peter II hair powder was introduced. Under Anne, for the first time officers wore uniforms of the same style as the soldiers with the addition of gold or silver lace, and they carried fusils. Uniforms became smarter and tighter; soldiers legs were encased in tight gaiters so hated by ordinary Russian soldiers whose national dress was loose. The predominant uniform colour of the army was green with red waistcoats, collars and cuffs and white cockades on hats. Sashes, still an important element in distinguishing national loyalties on the battlefield, were white, blue and red, later changed to black and gold. Sword knots were also black and gold. Dragoons had blue *kaftans*, red waistcoats' facings and trousers. Cuirassiers on service had *kaftans* like dragoons and tricornes with a protective metal *kaskett* inside. Their parade uniform, also often worn on campaign, comprised an elk-skin *collet* and trousers. The *collet* and the cuirass worn over it were trimmed with red cloth. The Life-Guard Horse Regiment was dressed in cuirassier uniform with the addition of gold lace.

The next logical step in the rehabilitation of the army was to go to war and who better to fight than Turkey again. With constant raids occurring across the border by freebooting Crimean tatars, excuses were not hard to find and in 1736 two armies under Field Marshal Münnich and Count Lacey invaded the Crimea. Militarily they were reasonably successful. They recaptured Azov and reached the Tatar capital but losses from privation rather than from battle were so heavy and the supply line so inefficient that they were forced to abandon their gains and withdraw back into Russia after devastating the countryside. In 1738 the offensive was renewed in the Crimea and Von Münnich's force this time attacked the Turkish Ukraine taking Ochakov though with heavy losses. In 1739 his target was Moldavia and here at last he had some real success defeating the Turkish army at the battle of Khotin. By the Treaty of Belgrade later that year, much of the Russian gains were returned but they kept Azov on condition that its fortifications were destroyed and also retained a large area of Turkish Ukraine.

The following year, Anne died and the short reign of Ivan under the regency of Anna Leopoldovnoa was ended by Peter's daughter, Elizabeth with yet another coup by the Guards. The new Empress acknowledged their part by giving the Grenadier Company of the Preobrajenski Regiment the title of 'Life Company' ennobling all ranks and appointing herself its Captain. To suit its new elevated position, the Company was separated from the regiment and given a gaudy uniform.

Under Elizabeth the reorganization of armed forces continued. The regular army created by her father was by now over forty years old, during which time it had accumulated considerable experience. It also included many good officers and some talented generals. Under their guidance military manuals were published and the artillery was reformed and rearmed. Russian traditional excellence in artillery dates from this period and in particular from the influence of its commander, Count Shouvalov.

There were, however, no great changes in dress or drill. In organization, the most noticeable change was in the number of light cavalry regiments. The newly conquered territories along the Black Sea provided a haven for the Sultan's persecuted Christians, Serbs, Moldavians, Greeks and others, all of whom were obliged in return to render military service and they were mostly formed into irregular and territorial hussar regiments.

Elizabeth's reign coincided with a period of turmoil in Western Europe, with a struggle for power between Frederick the Great's Prussia, Maria Theresa's Austria and the France of Louis XV. In the early stages, Britain at one end of Europe and Russia at the other end stood on the sidelines although as time went on they became more and more involved. During the War of the Austrian Succession, Elizabeth allied herself with Austria but took no very active part other than sending a small token force to join the army of George II, the main significance of which was that for the first time Russian soldiers were seen on the banks of the Rhine.

In 1756, Russia joined with Austria, France, Sweden and Saxony to oppose the growing power of Frederick the Great's Prussia. Frederick pre-empted the coalition by taking Saxony and invading Bohemia but he was repulsed by the Austrians. In June 1757, a Russian Army of 100,000 under Apraksin invaded East Prussia and defeated the Prussians at the battle of Gross Jägersdorf. Only supply problems and Apraksin's inertia prevented their marching on Berlin. In October, Fermor, who had replaced Apraksin, invaded East Prussia and took Königsberg. At Elizabeth's special command, East Prussia was 'for ever' incorporated in Russia and all the population was made to swear allegiance to her. Again in 1758, the Russians attacked, reaching the River Oder and on this occasion met Frederick himself at Zorndorf where they were halted after an indecisive battle. In 1759, the Russians, now led by Saltikov were more successful. After linking up with an Austrian army on the Oder, they defeated Frederick so severely at Kunersdorf that he contemplated abdication. Once again the Russians were unable to reap the full fruits of their victory because of inadequate supply services although in 1760, the Russians took Berlin, exacted a large indemnity and left again. During 1760–61, Frederick was able to keep superior Russian, Austrian and French armies at bay by dint of brilliant manoeuvring and forced marches but his strength was rapidly fading and it was apparent that he must soon face defeat. Then fate took a hand. On 25 December 1761, the Empress Elizabeth died suddenly. Her successor Peter III had always been a great friend and admirer of Frederick and was now able to demonstrate his affection by signing a generous peace, returning all conquered territories and even offering Frederick the loan of a Russian corps.

Peter III as ruling Duke of Schleswig Holstein had been allowed by Elizabeth to bring to Russia a Holstein corps and by 1762 this comprised seven infantry, two dragoon, three cuirassier and two hussar regiments. They were independent from the rest of the army and had their own uniform, organization and drill. Not unexpectedly they were regarded with some suspicion by the rest of the army and when, on his accession, Peter dressed the Imperial Guard like his Holsteiners, their suspicion formed an important factor in the guard's support of Catherine's successful coup. Peter died in captivity, probably murdered and his corps was allowed to return unmolested to Holstein.

The army which, in July 1762 swore allegiance to Catherine comprised four regiments of Imperial Guard (three infantry and one cavalry), fifty infantry regiments (including four grenadier regiments) and forty cavalry regiments including cuirassiers, horse grenadiers, dragoon and hussars. They were backed up by over eighty militia and garrison regiments and by artillery, howitzer, engineer and bridging units.

3
Catherine the Great 1762–1796 and Paul I 1796–1801

Catherine the Great

Catherine, although a German with no direct claim to the Russian throne came to power dedicated to freeing Russia from foreign influence and to the expansion of her territory. She even dreamt of placing her grandson Constantine on the throne in Constantinople as the new Byzantine Emperor. She was a typical disciple of 'enlightened absolutism', a combination of autocracy and progressiveness. In foreign policy she was a follower of Peter the Great who had solved the Baltic problem but had left the Black Sea problem unsolved and Catherine accomplished this with equal brilliance. Under the influence of Frederick the Great (who had sponsored her Russian marriage), she was also involved in three partitions of Poland which in the long run proved to be far less advantageous.

Conflict with Poland came early in her reign when a group of Polish noblemen (the Confederation of the Bar) organized a revolt against the Pro-Russian government but this merely invited Russian armed intervention and in 1772 came the first partition of Poland.

In 1768 Russian troops pursued the Poles into Turkish territory provoking the Turks into declaring war and invading the Ukraine. The first Turkish War of Catherine was generally successful for Russia. In 1769, Rumyantsov defeated the Turks on the banks of the Dniester and overran Moldavia and Wallachia. The following year they reached the Danube and in 1773, Souvorov inflicted a major defeat on the Turks at Shumla. Meanwhile Prince Dolgoruky had conducted a successful campaign in the Crimea. Fighting came to an end in 1773 when Russian troops were diverted to deal with the Pugachev revolt. By the treaty of 1774, Russia withdrew from the Balkans but retained the right to intervene there. They gained part of the Crimea, the Black Sea coast between the Bug and the Dnieper and the port of Azov.

Pugachev led a revolt of Ural cossacks promising to abolish serfdom and distribute land to the peasants. At the height of his success he had an army of 15,000 men, took the city of Kazan and came within 120 miles of Moscow. Souvorov was sent with reinforcements from the Danube but before he had reached the area, Pugachev had been betrayed and the revolt had collapsed.

In 1783, Catherine annexed the Crimea without opposition. In 1787, she demanded Georgia and Bessarabia from the Turks and the Second Turkish War began. After five years of fighting, mostly in the Balkans, the Russian armies under Potemkin and Souvorov had gained all territory to the East of Dniester, including the port of Odessa. This is still Russia's south-western border. Towards the end of the reign, Catherine again looked towards Poland. In 1793, in agreement with Prussia, she took most of Belorussia and the Polish Ukraine. In 1794, the Poles under Kosciusko rose in revolt but after some initial success, they were overwhelmed by the combined armies of Russia and Prussia. Poland was divided with Galicia going to Austria, Poznan and Warsaw to Prussia and all Belorussia to Russia. Catherine died in 1796 having realized most of her territorial aims.

Turning to the organization and dress of the army during Catherine's reign, her first act was to cancel the expensive uniform changes ordered by Peter III. She also abolished the Life Company returning its members to the Cavalier Guard which became a permanent body of sixty retained for ceremonial duties only and dressed in a neo-classical pantomimic style. She further augmented the Guard by the formation of a squadron of hussars and two *sotnias* of cossacks to be known as 'Hussars and Cossacks of the Imperial Court'.

To prepare the ground for any further changes which might be necessary, a military commission was set up in 1762 and this continued to sit throughout the reign. One of its early acts was, in 1773, to issue the first uniform regulations which standardized colour and embellishments while leaving the general style relatively unaltered. The uniform coat was to be green of a lighter shade with red facings, waistcoat and trousers. General officers were to have laurel leaf embroidery on cuffs and lapels. Brigadiers to have one narrow line, Major-Generals one broad, Lieut.-Generals one narrow and one broad and Generals one narrow and two broad. Field Marshals were also to have embroidery on sleeves and seams.

At regimental level, field officers had gold braid on hats, waistcoats and shabraques, one narrow and one broad line for full Colonels, one broad line for Lieut.-Colonels and Majors. Captains wore silver gorgets with a gold rim and subalterns, plain silver gorgets. Small epaulettes worn on the left shoulder were introduced, gold or silver for officers and wool for soldiers. These were like sword-knots in appearance and since the detailed design was left to the Colonel of the Regiment, some element of regimental distinction was allowed. One change introduced by Peter III which was allowed to remain was the black and orange cockade. Grenadier companies wore their distinctive hats and fuze-cases on their crossbelts. In 1765, in line with the trend throughout European armies, light infantry commands of sixty men were introduced into infantry regiments. The idea prospered and in due course separate light infantry regiments appeared. The uniform of the artillery was changed from red to green with black facings and later in Catherine's reign, horse artillery was introduced.

The administration and training of the army was improved by the introduction of a general staff quartermaster's department and by the formation of separate artillery and engineer cadet schools. A cadet school for children of Guard officers was formed and attached to the Life-Guard Ismailovski Regiment.

In 1769 a St Petersburg Legion of 5,000 men and a Moscow Legion of 10,000 men were formed but by 1775, having no obvious role, they were dispersed. There was a continuing expansion of irregular light cavalry formed from Christian subjects of the Sultan and by the end of Catherine's reign there were Don, Ural, Grebenski, Terek, Volga, Orenburg, Slobdski, Ukrainian, Zaparogski, Stavropol, Kalmuk, Astrakhan, Azov and Bachmut cossacks. They were permitted some individuality in dress but in general were largely influenced by Ukrainian cossacks with their familiar tall fur caps and *kaftans*.

In 1786, Prince Potemkin, a favourite of Catherine's was appointed

Viceroy of the newly conquered territories of the Black Sea and the Ukraine and he formed there a new corps with its own distinctive drill, manoeuvres and uniform. The tricorne hat was replaced by a helmet with black felt skull, a metal plate at the front and a band of coloured cloth at the back. Powdered hair and plaits were abolished and hair was cut short. The main garment was a *kurtka*, a short jacket of Polish origin. Trousers were loose and below the knee were reinforced with leather. Equipment was of black leather. The new uniform was at first for rank and file, the officers retaining their traditional uniforms except when on campaign. Gradually this new style of uniform was spread to all other units except the Guard, until Catherine's son Paul came to the throne with other ideas. The whole episode parallels the introduction of simpler and more practical uniforms by the British in America and the subsequent reaction after the loss of America.

As the Zesarevich Paul was strictly speaking the rightful holder of the throne after his father's death, Catherine had kept him at arm's length and allowed him no influence in matters of government. In other respects she allowed him a fairly free hand and did not seem worried at the prospect of him developing a power base of his own. She gave him the suburban palace estates of Pavlovsk and Gatchino and she raised no objections when he began to build up his own regiments and what was officially described as the Gatchino Corps (but which was colloquially referred to as 'Dad's Army' because of the way in which Paul emulated the Holstein Corps of his father). The Gatchino Corps was started in 1782 when Paul, who had received from the Empress the office of Grand Admiral; began to siphon off men from the Baltic naval battalions to form his own guard. At first only thirty men were involved but by 1785 they had become a full company and by 1788, a battalion. In 1786, cavalry and artillery were added and by the time of his accession to the throne ten years later, the corps comprised three battalions of infantry, regiments of cuirassiers, dragoons and hussars, a command of Don cossacks some fifty strong and an artillery company of 200 men with fifty-nine cannon. The personnel were at first transferred from other units but later they were re-enlisted or recruited from scratch.

The Corps was organized, drilled and clothed in a completely different way from the rest of the army. Paul's aim was to introduce the Prussian system, but he chose the system of Frederick the Great which was by then some twenty-five years out of date. Clothing was much tighter fitting with jackets buttoned down the front (half-way in summer, fully in winter) and gaiters, always unpopular with Russian soldiers. His grenadiers wore caps of Prussian style with metal plates and he even adopted the Prussian motto of 'Gott Mit Uns'. He also introduced a *Kaiserflagge*, reminiscent of the British Union Jack, and a cockade of black and orange, the Holstein colours, to which was later added white. His infantry, dragoons and artillery wore green. Cuirassiers wore steel cuirasses over white *collets* with red collars and cuffs, light blue leather trousers and top boots. Hussars wore a white dolman with light blue facings and pelisse, blue and white barrel sash, black fur cap with light blue bag and natural coloured leather trousers. Cossacks wore blue kaftans over red waistcoats, light blue trousers and black astrakhan caps with red bags. The hussars and cossacks survived Paul's death to become the guard regiments of hussars and cossacks. The Gatchino artillery were run in a thoroughly professional manner by Arakcheyev later to become Alexander I's first minister.

One of the first acts of Paul's reign was the decree of 29 November 1796 which laid down new regulations for the armament and uniform of the army. This had the effect of introducing Gatchino-style uniforms for the whole army even to the extent of requiring that all soldiers should powder and plait their hair in the Prussian style.

On Paul's unilateral and illegal assumption of the Grand Mastership of the Maltese Order, the Maltese Cross began to be used as a badge by the army. In 1798, it replaced the *Kaiserflagge* on grenadier caps. In 1799 he formed from the Cavalier Guard a 'Guard Attached to the Person of the Grand Master' and adopted the Maltese Cross as their badge. They wore a new style helmet with a white cockade bearing a red cross, red supervests with a white cross and black sabretaches with gold crown and silver Maltese Cross.

During the whole of his reign, Paul's main driving force was his hatred of his mother and her methods and his only consistent policy was to undo anything which she had done. So far as the army was concerned he sought to tighten up the loose discipline which prevailed under Catherine which was probably justified but which he carried out in a temperamental and unbalanced way.

His foreign policy was equally unpredictable. In theory he preferred non-interference in the upheavals which were spreading across Europe in the wake of the French Revolution but he would then change his policy for apparently trivial reasons. Bonaparte aroused his enmity when the French occupied Malta. The reason for his interest there dated back to the partition of Poland in 1794 when Russia took over large estates belonging to the Maltese Order. Paul returned them to the Order and as a token of gratitude was made their Protector. The whole concept caught his fancy and he had himself appointed Grand-Master of the Order by a group of Polish nobles and French emigrés. When Malta was taken, Paul, as Grand-Master felt bound to oppose the 'anti-Christ' Bonaparte and so formed the second coalition with Austria and Britain.

Austria had been steadily losing ground to the French in Italy and early in 1799, Paul sent a corps under Souvorov to help. Within a few months he had won back almost all the territory gained by Bonaparte in 1796-7. In the autumn, it was planned that the Russians would drive the French out of Switzerland but in difficult terrain and unsupported by the Austrians, part of the Russian corps of Rimsky-Korsakov was defeated.

This infuriated Paul who terminated the Austro-Russian alliance and ordered the withdrawal of the Russian army. Souvorov accomplished the withdrawal brilliantly bringing the army home intact. Paul awarded him the rank of Generalissimus and ordered the same honours to be given him as to the Emperor himself, a unique award. However Souvorov died the same year.

Paul also honoured his obligations to the second coalition by providing two divisions to join a British expeditionary force under the Duke of York which in 1799 landed at Texel on the northern tip of Holland. However coordination proved difficult and after a few indecisive battles the force was withdrawn.

The following year the whole picture changed. Bonaparte was progressing towards autocracy and in Paul's eye was thereby gaining respectability. Bonaparte built on this goodwill by releasing all his Russian prisoners and returning them home. Then to Paul's dismay his supposed allies, the British, took Malta from the French and disarmed a Russian fleet in the area. He turned his wrath on the British and ordered all trade to be ceased, an unpopular policy at home as Russia had become very dependent on British trade. He ordered an army of 20,000 cossacks under Orlov to march on India but it only reached Central Asia before disintegrating.

This was Paul's last military enterprise. A conspiracy of Guards officers had formed under Count Pahlen, the Governor-General of St Petersburg. In March 1801, Paul was assassinated and his son Alexander was proclaimed Tsar.

4
Alexander I
1801–1825

Alexander I

Alexander I came to the throne on a wave of relief and popularity, a sane, rational, good-looking man who seemed such a contrast from his father. He responded by adopting a liberal approach to political matters. In so far as the army was concerned however, he was still very much under the influence of the style which his father had created at Gatchino. Throughout his life he and his brother Constantine would refer to do things 'like Gatchino', implying a combination of panache and efficiency. He therefore retained much that had been introduced in Paul's reign but he carried on in a more sensible, less erratic, way. He had no wish to return to the loose discipline of Catherine's reign but appreciated the national pride which she had created. Early on in his reign therefore he removed some of the more obvious Prussian influences in the organization and dress of the army so much loved by Paul. He returned to the system of naming regiments after Russian towns and provinces and created for the army a new smart but comfortable dress of his own creation incorporating the best of contemporary French and British features.

On the international side, Alexander was wary of Napoleon but reluctant to become involved in Western Europe. However he became convinced that Russia was at risk from Napoleon's ambition and ruthlessness and in 1805 he joined Britain, Austria and Sweden in the third coalition. The allies planned to defeat the French in Italy and then attack north of the Alps. However Napoleon, in one of his most brilliant campaigns, surrounded and captured an Austrian army at Ulm and took Vienna. Having effectively split the allies, he concentrated on the Russo-Austrian army officially under Koutousov but in reality under Alexander's direct orders and decisively defeated them at Austerlitz. Alexander narrowly escaped with his life and the Russians withdrew to their own borders leaving the Austrians to capitulate.

After the defeat of Austria came the turn of Prussia. Politically the position was bizarre as Prussia had simultaneously concluded alliances both with France and Russia and the question was which of the two she would betray. In September 1806 Prussia presented an ultimatum to Napoleon demanding the withdrawal of all French troops from Germany. Napoleon responded by invading Prussia which was defeated in eight days and on 27 October, Napoleon entered Berlin. Russia which was officially still in a state of war with France and in accordance with the terms of her agreement with Prussia, ordered General Beningsen to cross the border with his Corps. Full of confidence, Napoleon had decided to carry on into Poland but he failed to take into account the hazards of a winter campaign on his extended supply lines. After some preliminary skirmishes, the two armies met in February 1807 at Preussisch Eylau, where after a bloody battle fought in appalling conditions, the French advance was halted in front of Königsberg. However in June 1807 the Russian Army was caught on the banks of the River Aller and was decisively defeated at Friedland. Alexander authorized Beningsen to conclude an armistice with the French which was readily accepted by Napoleon who in any case had no intention of crossing the Niemen and invading Russia.

Alexander now changed his policy and decided upon an accord with Napoleon. The Emperors met on a raft in the middle of the River Niemen and the Treaty of Tilsit was signed. Prussia gave up her share of Poland which became the Grand Duchy of Warsaw and her army was reduced to 40,000 men. Russia agreed to give Napoleon a free hand in Western Europe and to observe the continental system by ceasing trade with Britain. In return Russia received a free hand in Finland and Moldavia. After Tilsit Alexander went through a period of great unpopularity at home. Russians felt that he had signed a humiliating peace and the loss of British trade caused much hardship. However he needed a breathing space to study carefully the elements of Napoleon's success and to build up and improve his army. Meanwhile he undertook campaigns against Russia's traditional enemies. In 1808–09 he annexed Finland from Sweden and between 1809 and 1812 he fought the Turks, a war which was ended by the Treaty of Bucharest by which Russia gained Bessarabia.

Gradually relations with Napoleon deteriorated. Russia's observance of the continental system lapsed and in 1812, Britain persuaded Alexander to renounce it altogether. Napoleon decided that the time had come to stop Russian interference in European politics and to effect this he concentrated in Poland an army of over half a million men composed of Frenchmen, Italians, Germans and many other nationalities. Austria and Prussia were compelled to provide auxiliary corps which did little actual fighting. The Russians had two armies under Bagration and Barclay de Tolly concentrated on her western borders and in the early stages these narrowly escaped encirclement by the French. Alexander was reluctantly persuaded to leave the army to organize the defence of Russia and the raising of new armies and Koutousov was recalled from retirement to take overall command. He continued the retreat, halted to fight the fierce but indecisive battle of Borodino and then abandoned Moscow to the French, withdrawing the main Russian army to the south. Alexander meanwhile organized the raising of the *opolchenie*, a territorial volunteer force largely paid for by private contributions with most towns and provinces raising units. The *opolchenie* fought as formed units but also played a major role in providing reinforcements for regular regiments and in transport, pioneer and medical roles.

Napoleon now found himself in a most difficult position. He could advance further east but Russia stretched that way as far as China. If he advanced north to St Petersburg, he would have Koutousov behind him. If he advanced against Koutousov (now much strengthened by fresh troops) he would have Count Wittgenstein's Corps behind him. He would have chosen the south but did not have the strength to break through Koutousov and gain access to the southern regions hitherto unaffected by war. Finally, worried by the onset of bad weather, he decided to retreat along the same devastated route by which he had come. Harassed by Russian irregulars and then by atrocious weather conditions, his army disintegrated and was virtually wiped out. Koutousov was reluctant to pursue the French beyond the borders of Russia but he died leaving Alexander in sole charge.

He gambled on Prussia and Austria, both of whom were still nominally allies of Napoleon, changing sides. Prussia came over first and reorganized her army with Russian help and influence in matters of organization and dress. Six months later, Austria also joined with Schwarezenburg taking nominal command of the allied armies. In October 1813 the Battle of Leipzig (the 'Battle of the Nations') was fought over three days ending in Napoleon's retreat. Over the following six months he fought a series of brilliant rearguard actions but the overwhelming strength of the allies made the outcome inevitable. In April 1814, Napoleon abdicated and Alexander triumphantly led the allied armies into Paris. With the restoration of the Bourbon monarchy, the Russian army set off home. Their journey was interrupted in the spring of 1815 by the news of Napoleon's return from Elba, but after his defeat by the British and Prussians at Waterloo, they continued home.

Alexander's last decade was marked by reaction. With Napoleon's departure, he had become the most powerful leader in Europe and he advocated a Holy Alliance of monarchs, an early form of United Nations but with overtones of absolutism. At home, with the war over, the Gatchino influence was felt again. The army was smartened, uniforms tightened and drill became more rigid and formal. In 1816, he introduced the system of military settlements, whereby soldiers lived on the land and had to tend it while still maintaining their equipment and drill to the highest level. The system was unpopular since too much was asked of the men and after several mutinies had been brutally suppressed, it was abolished by Nicholas I.

The uniform of the army changed little during Alexander's reign, although appearance and style varied with the influences of fashion, war and peace. During the early years of his reign, 1801–05, Alexander concentrated on eliminating out-dated Prussian elements and on standardizing dress. By 1805 therefore, infantry soldiers wore a dark-green coat with red lining showing on the turnbacks, two rows of buttons down the front and collar and cuffs of regimental facing colour. Caps and bicorns had been replaced in 1803 by a tall felt shako with leather peak, black horsehair plume and a cockade on the front. The grenadier cap was abolished for all regiments except the Pavlovski Regiment who, as a mark of distinction for their conduct at Friedland retained them into modern times. The First Company still wore caps actually worn at the battle complete with bullet holes and the names of the original owners embossed on them. Trousers were white, cloth for winter and linen for summer, worn over black leather boots. Hair was worn short tied in a queue (until 1806) and powdered on special occasions. Equipment was of black leather and for winter wear the soldier wore a long browny-grey greatcoat or *shinel* which became a firm favourite, almost a replacement for the old *kaftan*. Senior officers wore cocked hats with a black feather plume and black, gold and white cockade, gold braid around their shoulder straps and gorgets in gilt metal for field officers and silver for subalterns. Junior officers carried spontoons.

Cavalry in 1805 comprised cuirassiers, dragoons, hussars and horse (later to be formed into lancers). Cuirassiers and dragoons wore similar black leather helmets with black horsehair crests except for officers whose crests were white with an orange and black tip. A brass plate with stamped eagle (St Andrew's star for guards) covered the front of the helmet. Cuirassiers had white collets with collar and cuffs of facing colour but as yet no cuirasses. Dragoons were, apart from the helmet, dressed like infantry. Hussars wore traditional hussar uniform with shakos like infantry. Lancers were developed around two regiments of light horse, the Polish and the Lithuanian. Alexander gave them a Polish-style uniform subsequently much copied by the French and other armies. This included the *confederatka*, a square-topped peakless cap which in 1803 was formalized into a *czapska*, a blue jacket or *kurtka* with plastrons, turnbacks and piping on seams. Officers wore silver epaulettes. Lance pennants were mainly red and blue with variations in arrangement according to regiment. Foot artillery and engineers wore infantry style uniforms with black facings and horse regiments followed the style of dragoons including crested helmets. This basic uniform altered little although headdress and trimmings were altered at three periods, 1807–09, 1812 and 1817.

In 1807–09 the shako (now known as the *kiver*) was covered with leather and reinforced with chevrons on the side. The cockade was replaced by a metal grenade with a single flame for infantry and three flames for grenadiers. Guard infantry regiments adopted the double-headed eagle as a shako plate. The large plume was replaced by a pompom for all except guard regiments. The shako was also now worn by officers with black and orange cords and a silver pompom. Hussars and artillery conformed with these changes. Officers' shoulder straps were replaced by epaulettes with fringes for field officers and without for junior officers. Gorgets were reduced in size. The round helmet crest of cuirassiers, dragoons and horse artillery was replaced by a flattened black horsehair fringe.

In 1812 the shape of the shako was altered, it became lower and was given a concave top. Collars became lower and looser. Cuirassiers were given black cuirasses with red edging. These were supplied also by the Russians to the Prussian army and were retained by them into modern times. Mounted rifle regiments were introduced, clothed like dragoons but with shakos instead of helmets. The *opolchenie* formed in 1812 wore virtually peasant costume of long coats of all shades of grey and beige, trousers tucked into loose boots and a round peaked cap of cloth or fur. Their only universal item of uniform was the brass cross with the Imperial cypher in the centre, sewn on to the cap. This was adopted in 1813 by the Prussian *Landwehr* and became the pattern for the Iron Cross, the Prussian war decoration. Cossacks continued with their traditional dress although as the war progressed, attempts were made to standardize and most followed the Don cossack dress of dark blue *kaftan* with red facings, blue baggy trousers and astrakhan cap with red bag. Cossacks of the Guard wore a red *demi-kaftan* with white braid down the collar and front.

After 1817, the *kiver* was heightened again and stiffened. A new shako plate was introduced based on the design worn by the British in their Waterloo shako (pattern 1812–16), stamped with a St Andrew's star. Insignia of distinction were introduced, initially in the form of an amazon shield worn above the shako plate, later replaced by a scroll. Dragoons changed their helmets for *kivers*. Hussars and lancers also adopted the new shako plate but horse artillery deviated from the others by having a badge of crossed cannon. Guard infantry retained their shako plates of double-headed eagles and their long plumes. Another significant change was the introduction of plastrons of regimental facing colour for guard, grenadier and jaeger regiments. These have been retained into modern times and are still worn with ceremonial dress by Soviet guard units. Variations from this would occur in the future but the uniforms of Alexander I's reign set the traditional pattern of Russian uniform.

5
Nicholas I
1825–1855

The reign of Nicholas I began in peculiar circumstances. Alexander I had no direct heir and strictly speaking the next in line was his brother, Constantine, commander-in-chief in Poland. It had been agreed for some time that he did not want to leave Poland and that he would renounce the succession in favour of Nicholas but nothing had been officially decreed. When the time came, Nicholas, followed by the army and the government, swore allegiance to Constantine and Nicholas refused to make any move without formal confirmation of renunciation from him. In the later reactionary years of Alexander's reign, a number of secret societies had sprung up among officers led by those who had campaigned through Europe in 1813–15 and had seen something of life under more liberal regimes. A group in St Petersburg decided that they could exploit the interregnum and Nicholas' hesitation to introduce a constitutional monarchy or republic, according to their varying political aims, and they decided that this could best be done by publicly proclaiming their loyalty to Constantine.

Eventually it became clear that Nicholas was to accept the throne and plans were made for the Guard to swear allegiance to the new Tsar on 14 December 1825 on the Senate Square. The conspirators

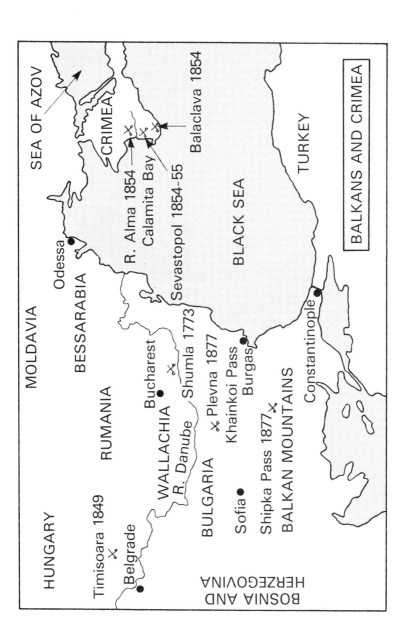

BALKANS AND CRIMEA

HUNGARY

MOLDAVIA

SEA OF AZOV

CRIMEA

RUMANIA

BESSARABIA

Odessa

R. Alma 1854

Calamita Bay

Sevastopol 1854-55

Balaclava 1854

Timisoara 1849

Belgrade

WALLACHIA

Bucharest

R. Danube

Shumla 1773

BLACK SEA

BOSNIA AND HERZEGOVINA

BULGARIA

Sofia

Plevna 1877

Khainkoi Pass

Shipka Pass 1877

BALKAN MOUNTAINS

Burgas

Constantinople

TURKEY

decided that this was their moment and they came to the Square with their units having explained to the soldiers that it was their sacred duty to be firm in their allegiance to the true Tsar, Constantine, and that they should refuse to take the oath to the 'usurper' Nicholas. Nicholas himself came down to the Square supported by the Preobrajenski Guard, Horse Guards and Cavalier Guards. For much of the day the opposing groups stood facing one another with periodic verbal exchanges. At length Nicholas ordered up artillery and the conspiracy was ended by a few rounds of grapeshot. Now unchallenged, he assumed the throne and took due vengeance on the conspirators.

The guiding force of Nicholas' reign was his infatuation with his brother. To the best of his ability, he followed Alexander's system and the first consideration in arriving at any decision was how Alexander would have dealt with the problem. But he was a different character, simpler, less intelligent, but more consistent and pedantic, personally attending to every detail. His education had had a military bias and from early manhood he lived the life of a regular army officer, in command first of the Guard Sapper Battalion, then of the 1st Guard Division and he carried out other military duties which he performed with the utmost diligence to the detriment of his popularity. He was tall, good-looking with a marvellous figure for uniform and had very pale blue eyes with which he would fix those whom he addressed with an icy stare. He was reactionary and lacked tact. For example his brother always wore the British Order of the Garter around his Order of St Andrew, the premier Russian order. Nicholas instead relegated it to be worn on his Order of St Vladimir. This lack of tact was to be one of the factors which led up to the Polish Uprising of 1831 and, later, the Crimean War.

He was a good organizing functionary. He abolished Alexander's military settlements because they did not work. He established military training colleges, took a detailed interest in military organization and drills and spent much of his time travelling around the country paying unexpected visits to military establishments. Worried by a possible repetition of the Decembrists' rising, he formed the 'third section' of his secretariat to act as a large and efficient secret police organization.

But in military matters, Nicholas lacked imagination and creativity. He encouraged officers cast in his own mould, unimaginative and concerned with detail as personified by his two leading generals,

Diebitsch and Paskevitch. As a result his army, although superbly organized on paper, did not progress in matters of equipment and tactics and gradually fell behind the other armies of Europe.

In the early years of his reign, Russia seemed all powerful and impregnable. With the defeat of Napoleon, no other European power could challenge her and Alexander had thwarted possible rivalry by his Holy Alliance with Prussia and Austria. Nicholas took advantage of this to continue Russian expansion at the expense of the Turks. Alexander had been against the liberation of the Christian subjects of the Sultan because that encouraged rebellion against established authority, but Nicholas felt no such qualms. He had inherited from his brother a dispute with Persia over border areas which led to a war lasting from 1825 to 1828, the climax coming in 1827 with the storming of Erivan which left the Russians in a position to threaten Teheran. Persia sued for peace, paying an indemnity and giving up the disputed border provinces.

In 1828, Nicholas moved against Turkey, nominally in support of Greek independence but with an opportunity for further territorial gains much in mind. His army attacked on two fronts, across the Danube led by Nicholas himself and in the Caucasus. The campaign of 1828 failed, but in 1829 the Russian army was more successful and when peace came in September 1829, they retained the mouth of the Danube and the eastern coast of the Black Sea. Russia also obtained guarantees of the independence of Greece and the autonomy of Moldavia and Wallachia. Von Moltke, the great German military theorist, writing on this campaign, considered that the Russian army had done well in spite of poor equipment and supplies and ill health and that its great asset was the courage and high morale of its soldiers.

In 1830, encouraged by the July revolution in France, a group of Polish radicals rose against Russia. Constantine narrowly escaped with his life thanks to the Russian garrison of Warsaw which succeeded in extricating him and concentrating outside the city. The revolt spread and early in 1831, Nicholas sent in the Russian army under Paskevitch. After six months of fierce fighting, the Russians eventually retook Warsaw, the remnants of the Polish army slipped over into East Prussia where it was disarmed and the war ended. The overwhelming strength of the Russians made the outcome inevitable, but Paskevitch (now Prince of Warsaw), the archetype of

Nicholas' rigid, unimaginative type of officer was established as the head of the Russian army for the remainder of his reign.

Apart from continuing expansion in the Caucasus, the next seventeen years were peaceful and stable, but beneath this deceptive exterior, the power of the absolute monarchies was beginning to wane. In 1848 they faced their greatest threat since 1789. The King of France was replaced, the throne of Prussia tottered and the Hapsburg dynasty faced revolt in Italy in the south and Hungary and Czechoslovakia in the east. Only the thrones of Britain and Russia remained steady. Hungary had declared independence under Kossuth but the Czechs' attempt to follow suit was suppressed by the Austrian army in June 1848. Encouraged by their success, they invaded Hungary in September 1848 but were repulsed and thrown back towards Vienna; they attacked again and early in 1849 were repulsed again. Nicholas decided that the time had come for Russia to step in and with the famous watchword 'Submit Yourselves, Ye Peoples, for God is with Us', sent in from the north an army of 100,000. They linked up with the Austrians and at the Battle of Timisoara in August 1849, the Hungarians were defeated.

With Europe quiet again, and, in Nicholas' view, in his debt for his efforts in quelling revolution, he decided that the time was ripe once more for war with Turkey and on this occasion he used as pretext a conflict over the rights of access to the Holy Places of Jerusalem. However the Western Powers were rightly suspicious of Russian intentions and to his anger and dismay, Nicholas was faced with the threat of war from France, Britain and Austria who in Nicholas' words 'astonished the world by her ingratitude', although in the event she remained on the sidelines.

In 1853, Russia annexed Moldavia and Wallachia and France and Britain declared war in March 1854. By the time the allied expeditionary force had been shipped to the area and were ready for action, fighting between the Russians and Turks was virtually over, but the allies still decided to go ahead and in September 1854 they landed in the Crimea. The Russians were thrown back from the Alma and the allies would probably have been able to take Sevastopol with little trouble if they had pressed on, but in the event the Russians were given time to fortify it and were able to hold out for nearly a year before abandoning it. A negotiated peace followed soon after and the allies withdrew from the area. Although Russia's defeat had no great significance, it struck greatly at her pride that an invading force had been allowed to remain on Russian territory for so long and that the Russian army had failed to dislodge it. The army was shown up as a paper tiger. Magnificent in review and on the pages of the military print publisher, but backward in armaments, supplies and communications and with ineffective commanders.

Nicholas I accepted blame, realized peace negotiations were called for, but was too proud to accept the facts. He took the only remaining course open to him. He attended a review in mid-winter inadequately protected, refused to have his subsequent illness treated and died of pneumonia, leaving the fate of Russia in the hands of his son, Alexander II.

In matters of uniform, as in other matters relating to the army, the main feature of Nicholas' reign was lack of change. He introduced a few changes early on in his reign. The double-breasted jacket was replaced by a single-breasted version. White trousers were replaced by dark green except for summer parade wear. In 1828, the English-style shako plates worn by line infantry, dragoons and lancers were replaced by double-headed eagles. Regimental numbers were worn on head-dress plates and buttons and divisional numbers on shoulder boards.

The most important change came in 1844–5 when the pickelhaube or spiked helmet was introduced. Nicholas I designed this himself basing it on the traditional Slavonic helmet which was often featured in architectural motifs and other art forms. The story goes that Frederick William IV of Prussia saw an early prototype when on a visit to Nicholas and asked if he could borrow it. He decided that it should be adopted for the Prussian army also, and being rather more efficient in such matters, the Prussian army had it available for issue in 1843, a year earlier than the Russians. Interestingly enough, the British Household Cavalry, probably through the influence of Prince Albert, introduced a similar helmet in 1842 which they still wear today.

The helmet which probably more than any other symbolizes the Russian and Prussian empires, the metal helmet surmounted by an eagle was a combined effort. Nicholas I, as always with economy in mind, decided first that the existing crested helmets of cuirassiers could be adapted by removal of the crests and substitution of an eagle for guard regiments and a spike in the form of a grenade for line regiments. Presumably the results were not satisfactory as within a year a metal helmet with lobster tail like the Prussian model had been introduced.

Infantry, dragoons and corps were issued with a leather pickelhaube with a grenade for everyday wear embellished with a plume for parades. Hussars retained their shakos except for the Guard Hussars who adopted a fur busby.

In 1848, a new uniform was laid down for the Caucasian Corps, a separate autonomous organization less rigidly controlled from the centre than the rest of the army and therefore a breeding ground for ideas and experiment. It was similar in this respect to the British-Indian army. The uniform which was introduced was the forerunner of that adopted throughout the army under Alexander II and was much influenced by the dress of cossacks and the tribes which the army had encountered in the Caucasus. The head-dress was a fur cap with no badges except honour scrolls and, in warm weather, peaked caps with large peaks. The coatee was replaced by a *demi-kaftan* or tunic with upturned collar. Epaulettes were often discarded as too cumbersome and officers were distinguished by their *contre-epaulettes*. Trousers were worn tucked into long soft boots.

Equipment was modernized. The *porte-epée* holding the infantry soldier's sword was replaced by a belt with a frog and the sword itself was replaced by a saw-edged version previously only used by sappers with the bayonet worn in the same scabbard. White leather equipment was blackened and a lightweight haversack was introduced. In place of the old cartridge pouch, a bandolier with space for sixty rounds was introduced.

The emergence of the Romantic movement had its effect here and in the development of the more exotic Circassian style dress which was encouraged by Nicholas I and which again had its parallel in the appearance of traditional Indian dress in the uniforms of British-Indian irregular cavalry. In the Russian army they were confined to a limited number of special units and individuals.

During the early stages of the Crimean War, in April 1854, an order was issued simplifying officers' campaign dress. Among other points, this laid down that officers should wear soldiers' style *shinels* or greatcoats. Epaulettes were proving too visible to enemy marksmen and in their place officers' shoulder boards or *pogoni* were introduced and remain a distinctively Russian feature of uniform to the present day. They began as soldiers' cloth shoulder straps with officers' braid sewn on according to rank. Generals had one broad band of zig-zag pattern hussar braid, field officers three lines of sword-sling braid and junior officers two lines. Rank stars were also worn as on epaulettes. In other respects the uniform worn by Russian soldiers during the war did not vary much from regulation. The pickelhaube was soon found to be unsuitable for action and they were discarded in favour of forage caps. Hussars with shakos and cossacks with fur caps both wore versions made from waterproof covers. The *shinel* was found to be too long and was generally worn with the skirts gathered up.

6
Alexander II
1855-1881

The accession of Alexander II in 1855 was overshadowed by the failure of the Russian army in the Crimea and he inherited the tasks of making peace with the allies and rectifying the shortcomings of the army. In the Crimea, the allies whose military difficulties had been almost as great as those of the Russians, were in the mood for peace. Sevastopol had been taken, Napoleon III had made the point that his regime and army were to be respected and there was little else to be done. The peace terms signed at the Treaty of Paris were not therefore over-harsh. The Black Sea was to be neutralized and no naval activity by any power was to take place there; a portion of Bessarabia was returned to Moldavia which together with Wallachia and Serbia were made autonomous vassals of the Sultan; the interests of the Turkish Christians were to be protected by the Western European powers rather than by Russia. None of these clauses had any lasting effect.

The question of reform of the army was much more complex and difficult to resolve since it was tied to the need for political reform. Alexander II while tall and distinguished and looking every inch a monarch, was more benevolent, less rigid than his father. He had been under the influence of liberal ideas from an early age and was prepared to be persuaded that the time had come for some liberal ideas to be implemented. His main decision, taken in the face of much opposition from Russia's landowning classes was that the serfs should be liberated. This was not a purely humanitarian measure, but was linked with the need to reform the army. The soldiers who made up the army of Nicholas I were long service men, who served from twenty to twenty-five years and were then pensioned off to garrison and veteran establishments. This system had provided a smart, well-disciplined and trained regular army but, as the war had shown, there was no reserve available and if a war escalated to the point where the regular army could not cope, the only alternative was to raise new regiments of young, untrained recruits. The only alternative, already adopted in many other European countries, was conscription, whereby a high proportion of young men served for a limited period and were then held on a reserve liability. But Russia could only introduce conscription by liberating the serfs.

This all took time to implement. The Imperial *Ukase* announcing the liberation of the serfs was signed on 9 February 1861, but the accompanying military reforms were not implemented until the Decree of 1 January 1874, which laid down that all Russian men at the age of 21 were obliged to perform personal military service without any right of replacement excepting only criminals. Part of this service was to be with the active army (three years in the infantry, four years in other arms) and part with the reserve (fifteen and thirteen years respectively). Finally there was a continuing commitment to serve with the *opolchenie*. In the event, not all those available were required to serve. In 1875 of 700,000 eligible only 150,000 were called, the rest going straight to the reserve. Exemption from active service on educational or economic grounds could be obtained, although there was then a more rigorous reserve liability. Those with educational qualifications were encouraged to volunteer for active service in return for special status and privileges and, after service, they usually qualified as officers in the reserve.

This change in pattern in the army did not result in any particular change in the order of battle of the regular army, which remained about 500,000 strong, but because of the increased turnover of personnel, training facilities had to be expanded and many more officers' schools were opened.

This was also a period when technological advances were beginning to take effect and this was reflected in the expansion of the technical arms.

In his foreign policy, Alexander continued the pattern of his predecessors, maintaining the *status quo* in the west and looking for opportunities for expansion in the south-west, south-east and east. In Central Asia his armies took Bokhara and Turkestan, Transcaspia becoming part of the Russian Empire. Russia had reached the borders of Afghanistan providing a fresh and continuing worry for the British Government and its representative commander-in-chief in India. From China, Russia was ceded territory which became the Maritime Province where the naval base of Vladivostock was founded.

But still in Russian eyes the main target was the ailing Ottoman Empire and its domination over the Christian populations of the

Balkans. When therefore in 1875, Christian uprisings in Herzegovina and Bosnia were cruelly suppressed by the Turks, the strength of reaction in Russia led inexorably to war. However the Western Powers remained firmly opposed to the possibility of Russia gaining an outlet to the Mediterranean. Austria and England put as a condition of their neutrality that there should be no annexation of Constantinople and no territorial acquisition by Russia. Even with the possibility of ultimate gain pre-empted, Russia nevertheless declared war on Turkey in April 1877.

In June, the Russians with an army of 250,000 seized the crossings of the Danube and a mobile force under General Gourko captured the vital Khainkoi pass through the Balkans, forcing the Turks to abandon the more important Shipka Pass. If the Russian army had consolidated these gains quickly they would have had Constantinople at their mercy there and then. However Imperial Headquarters was worried by the threat of Osman Pasha's army in their rear and when he unexpectedly recaptured Plevna, an important fortress and road junction, the main Russian army was diverted to retake it. Initial assaults gallantly led by General Skoboleff, failed at considerable cost and a full siege became necessary which lasted five months before Osman Pasha surrendered on 10 December 1877. The Russians even nearly lost the vital Shipka Pass when a Turkish counter-attack found the garrison much reduced but it held out until reinforced.

With Plevna captured, the Russians were at last able to carry the campaign over the Balkans and, in January 1878, in a series of engagements, the remaining Turkish field armies were defeated and the Russians halted before the walls of Constantinople, now protected by the British fleet. An armistice followed and in March, the Treaty of San Stefano was signed by which Russia recovered the parts of Bessarabia and Kars, lost after the Crimean War and Turkey conceded the independence of Montenegro, Serbia, Roumania and Bulgaria. However the Western Powers intervened and in Berlin the following July, the terms were modified particularly with regard to Bulgaria, part of which remained under Turkish protection with the remainder becoming an independent principality. Alexander was much criticized by the Panslavist element in Russia for these concessions and the general air of dissatisfaction and malaise which set in was exploited by the revolutionary element. Three years of assassination attempts followed and the general unrest came to a climax in March 1881 when Alexander was fatally wounded by a bomb thrown at him while on his way to sign a manifesto granting Russia a constitution.

Changes in the uniform of the army during Alexander II's reign followed the general trend of European armies of the time for 'Le Confort Français', a looser, easier style developed by the French army in Africa, with in Russia's case the corresponding influence of the Caucasian Corps described in Chapter 5. The first major change of his reign had already been approved by Nicholas I before his death, the decree of 15 March 1855 which abolished the coatee in favour of the double-breasted tunic and introduced the shako for all except Generals and some guard regiments and cossacks who retained their own distinctive head-dress. Generals and officers of the suite of the Tsar adopted a white fur cap, the first appearance of what was to become a familiar Russian distinction. Honour swords were to be embellished with a sword knot of the ribbon of the Order of St George, the first association of Order and weapon. In May it was decreed that officers should wear light-grey *shinels* with *pogoni* in place of epaulettes.

The shako was worn only until 1864 when it was replaced by a lower, French-style kepi which was intended to replace both the shako and the undress forage cap or *furashka*. Inevitably there was considerable resistance to this French import, led by those regiments which had been allowed to retain their traditional head-dress. They soon received dispensation to go on with the *furashka* rather than adopt the kepi for undress. In 1872, a stiffer version of the kepi was introduced with gold braid around the top for officers in the Austrian style. Regiments continued to press for a return to more traditional Russian head-dress and by the Russo-Turkish war, the kepi was still worn only by the less fashionable line regiments. The double-headed eagle head-dress plate underwent various changes. By the Imperial Ukase of 29 May 1857, the state eagle emblem was changed to the 'wings up' position and shako plates were altered accordingly to the new style eagle worn over a shield bearing the regimental number. Guard regiments adopted a larger eagle without shield. With the introduction of the kepi there was much less space for a plate and the shield was removed leaving the eagle on its own. In 1872 guard regiments began to wear the St Andrew's star over the eagle.

A steady flow of uniform changes throughout Alexander's reign continued in the direction of greater comfort and practicality combined with an element of Russification. The tunic, at first called a *polukaftan* was renamed *mundir* in 1859 and in 1872 was replaced by a single-breasted version. In 1860, white *gimnasterka* were introduced for general wear by soldiers, white jackets or *kitels* for officers and white linen covers over caps for all ranks on service. With the introduction of the kepi in 1862 came also the *bashlik* or hood for winter wear. In 1868 *pogoni* for wear with greatcoats and *kitels* were made detachable and in 1871 the custom began of adding the insignia of the arms to *pogoni* (with telegraphists leading the way). In 1868, breeches and boots in place of overalls became universal wear for campaigns and in 1873, soldiers began to wear greatcoats rolled over the shoulder instead of around the knapsack. Anticipating the wider changes in organization of the cavalry introduced later by Alexander III, army cuirassiers were designated dragoons and uniformed accordingly.

The Russian soldiers who bravely followed their beloved General Skoboleff in repeated charges against the defences of Plevna wearing soft kepis, shirts, rolled greatcoats and loose trousers tucked into boots, led by officers in white caps and jackets, looked very different from their fathers defending Sevastopol and were much closer to the image of the Russian soldier which we still have today.

7
Alexander III 1881–1894
and Nicholas II 1894–1917

The assassination of Alexander II brought to a close the most liberal regime that Russia has seen before or since but the atmosphere of reform encouraged by him was immediately stifled by his son Alexander III. His first manifesto dealt with the strengthening of autocracy. Reaction and suppression became the order of the day and remained so throughout his reign and that of his son, Nicholas II.

Unlike most of his predecessors, Alexander III had no particular interest in the army and preferred political to military affairs. He never called upon the army to fight during his reign although he used it increasingly for internal security to the detriment of its morale. What interest he did take was essentially reactionary. He maintained a tight grip on the military budget at a time when rapid technical development required ample funds for new weapons and equipment. He encouraged the return of the type of officer who flourished under Nicholas I, obedient, working by the book and with no originality or initiative. He imposed important changes in military education. Soldiers were no longer to be taught to read and write so that they would not be corrupted by revolutionary propaganda. The officers' military schools which under Alexander II had provided a good standard of general education reverted to cadet schools teaching principally military matters.

Alexander III also reacted against foreign influence in all walks of life, which, in the army, took the form of prejudice against officers of non-Russian origin and Russification of the appearance of the army. The latter changes took place with unusual speed, the whole army having been reclothed in the 'Russian peasant' style by his coronation in 1882. The pickelhaube and shako were both abolished leaving the *furashka* (peakless forage cap) for everyday wear and a new style of fur hats (*shapka*) for parades, requiring smaller cap eagles and St Andrew's stars. The main garment was a double-breasted tunic without buttons and fastened instead by hooks with a pleated back like a *kaftan*. Epaulettes, *pogoni* and embroidery on collar and cuffs

GULF OF FINLAND

EASTERN EUROPE

BALTIC SEA

Riga

Danzig

Königsberg

EAST
PRUSSIA

Masurian Lakes
1914

Minsk

Tannenberg 1914

POLAND

BELORUSSIA

Pripet Marshes

Warsaw

Brest Litovsk

Lublin

Lake Naruch 1916

Kiev

R. Dnieper

GERMANY

Lvov
(Lemburg)

R. Bug

AUSTRO-HUNGARY

CARPATHIAN

R. Dniester 1916

MOUNTAINS

R. Dniester

Odessa

RUMANIA

R. Danube

BLACK SEA

remained unaltered. Trousers, baggier than before, were tucked into knee-high boots. All line cavalry regiments were converted into dragoons and their uniforms standardized on the same lines as the infantry. Only the guard retained their traditional uniforms except for the L-G Dragoon Regiment. A single style of sword was chosen for use by all arms. In line with the general trend of Russification, this was a *shashka* with a Caucasian style blade and worn in the Caucasian manner hanging from a narrow belt over the right shoulder with the edge facing backward.

At the close of Alexander III's reign, the army totalled 820,000 men backed up by a reserve army of 275,000. There were 250 infantry regiments each of four battalions, including twelve guard, sixteen grenadier, 165 line, twenty rifle and thirty-seven Far Eastern regiments, with a further 136 regiments in reserve. The cavalry comprised ten guard, fifty-one dragoon and fifty-one cossack regiments. These were grouped into forty-eight infantry divisions and twenty-two cavalry divisions which in their turn formed twenty-two army corps.

Alexander's early death in 1894 and the accession to the throne of his son, Nicholas II, made little difference to the downward course of the Russian state and its army. Like his father, he was a reactionary, a firm believer in autocracy but he did not have the mental or physical strength of Alexander. He surrounded himself with ineffective ministers and generals and usually agreed with the last of them to whom he had spoken. He had no understanding of military affairs and in an age of increasing technology, considered military equipment and weapons to be of little importance. However, in spite of his attitude, the pressure of events forced changes and some modernization did eventually occur. What impetus there was came largely from the French, anxious to develop Russian strength to counterbalance that of Germany. A military treaty had been signed by Alexander III shortly before his death and Nicholas endorsed this by an exchange of visits with the French President. With the help of French capital, Russia began to industrialize and to develop her railway system. French military missions began the task of updating the army's weapons. It had, for example, been planned to re-equip the artillery entirely with the French 75 mm. gun by 1918, but this had only just started when war came.

But even if Nicholas had to be forced into modernizing his army, he still had ideas of expansion of his empire including plans to annex Manchuria and Korea, Tibet and Persia, and, like his predecessors, he had designs on Constantinople and the Bosphorus. For the most part, he was deterred from action by the risk of retaliation from the other European powers, except in the Far East where he felt less constrained since Russia's main rival there, Japan, was an unknown quantity. In common with other European powers, Russia had been able to move troops into China at the time of the Boxer rebellion in 1900 and she had also infiltrated Manchuria, bringing her to the borders of Korea, which Japan regarded as her domain. Seeing the vulnerability of Russia's forces in the Far East, the army dependent on the 5,000 mile Trans-Siberian railway and the fleet dependent on one ice-free harbour, Port Arthur, Japan attacked in February 1904 without warning. By sea after an initial attack on Vladivostock, Japan was content to blockade and gradually whittle down the Russian Far East Fleet. Port Arthur was besieged and despite several fierce attacks, held out for nearly a year before falling. Japanese armies invaded Manchuria, but after a series of indecisive battles, with heavy casualties on either side, they were unable to do more than gradually force the Russians back. In the end it was revolution at home and the destruction of the Russian Baltic Fleet which had made prodigious efforts to sail half-way around the world only to meet destruction at Tsushima, which brought the protagonists to the conference table. By the Treaty of Portsmouth (U.S.A.), Russia surrendered Port Arthur and evacuated Manchuria.

The main problem of the Russian army had been supply and communications. The Far Eastern Military District had been mobilized including the reserve and *opolchenie*. Transbaikal and East Siberian cossacks were used. Some troops were sent from Central and Western Russia, but they were limited by the capacity of the railways. As in the Crimea fifty years before, the command structure had become bureaucratic and indecisive. All too often the initiative lay with the Japanese who preferred to split their formation into independent commands. Both with the army and at home the war was unpopular from the start and became more so as the lack of success became apparent. Discontent finally came to the surface in the revolution of 1905, involving demonstrations, strikes and disruption of the railways, met by brutal retaliation from the police and army. Eventually Nicholas was forced to concede a constitution. Now, at last, some modernization began, helped by a burgeoning economy which showed signs of bringing real prosperity to the state, to the extent that by 1914, Russia was spending as much on her army as Germany.

But the degree and direction of the modernization of the army remained a matter for dispute. General Sukhomlinov, appointed war minister in 1908, was at the centre of the controversy. Although an old army establishment figure, he was sufficiently progressive to arouse opposition from the patrician wing of the army. For example he wished to reduce expenditure on fortresses and siege artillery in favour of artillery but was overruled. He found also that, although money was available, the technology and productivity of Russian industry could not yet cope with the demand. When war came in 1914, the deficiencies in planning were shown up. Russia had the men (114 divisions against 96 German) and the guns (6,700 to 6,000) and the railways to transport them but the guns were of the wrong type, soldiers were in the wrong place and the railways were taken up with too many cavalry horses and their fodder. Too little attention had been paid to reserves whether of men or ammunition.

In matters of uniform, the reign of Nicholas II produced the same combination of reaction and reluctant modernization. For the first ten years there was little change and the army went to war with Japan with white *kitels* for officers and white *gimnasterkas* and *furashkas* for soldiers in summer and fur *shapkas* and *shinels* for winter. However with the increasing fire-power and range of modern rifles, colour of uniform now mattered and white proved highly unsuitable. At first officers began adapting uniform, dyeing their white *kitels* khaki and having khaki *kitels* made privately in the 'English' style with patch pockets.

Immediately after the war, khaki was universally adopted. For summer wear soldiers wore the khaki *furashka*, linen *gimnasterka* and linen trousers tucked into boots. In winter they wore fur caps and greatcoats over wool shirts. Officers wore khaki *kitels*, linen for summer wear and cloth for winter. Parade uniforms remained the same except that in 1908 the fur *shapka* was abolished leaving only the *furashka*. Because this left no space for special regimental insignia such as honour scrolls, gorgets were reintroduced for those regiments entitled to such distinctions (numbering some 300). The tall fur cap with side flaps (*papaha*) was developed in 1910–11 but was only just fully introduced by 1914. With the *papaha* the double-headed eagle

47

badge and honour scrolls as appropriate were reintroduced for parade wear.

In 1907–08, dragoon regiments which had formerly been hussars and lancers reverted to their old roles and adopted the traditional full dress of Alexander II pattern with only the cut brought up to date. Former cuirassier regiments were given crested helmets like Horse Grenadiers without the back flap and *collets*, cuirassier-style tunic with braid down the front. The Life-Guard Imperial Family Rifles Battalion reverted to their Nicholas I-style uniform.

In 1908 a new full dress shako or *kiver* was introduced for general officers, guard infantry, grenadier regiments, guard dragoons, guard artillery and guard sappers. The badge was the St Andrew's star for guards and the double-headed eagle for line regiments. There was ample space for honour scrolls. At the same time, guard infantry reverted to a double-breasted tunic with plastron of facing colour of the regiment (*mundir*). In 1911–12, moves were begun to abolish parade uniforms for all except guard regiments and in their place to provide modifications to the standard khaki uniform. The *kitel* for example was provided with hook-on plastron, collar and cuffs of regimental colour and pattern. With this was worn the new *papaha* embellished with eagle and other distinctions. The infantry officer's sword reverted to the Alexander II style with metal scabbard and rings.

War put an end to these proposals before they had gone too far. With ten million men to clothe and an industry which found it virtually impossible to cope with the demands of modern war, uniform had to be kept simple. Summer wear remained the same as that introduced in 1906–07. In winter, the soldier was well provided with the new *papaha*, *shinel* made during war-time with hooks in place of buttons, and quilted jacket and trousers for wear underneath. Officers developed a variety of styles, the favourite being various modifications of the British Norfolk jacket. A steel helmet of French pattern with the Russian double-headed eagle applied, appeared in 1916 but it was never made in Russia and was not used on a particularly wide scale being reserved for special battalions serving in France and Salonika. As the war went on and shortages became more marked, uniformity and quality of dress deteriorated.

Russia entered World War I prepared to implement Plan 19 (revised), which had been settled in 1912. Forty-seven divisions were to concentrate against the Austrians and thirty divisions were to conduct a two-pronged offensive against the Germans in East Prussia, an equable distribution which in the event failed to provide decisive strength on either front. The plan of the Central Powers was for Germany to keep the bulk of her army on the Western front for a campaign which was only due to last six weeks while Austria bore the weight of the Eastern front. The Germans later modified this plan and left a larger force in East Prussia with the intention of going on the offensive there from the start.

In an unselfish act of support for the French, Russia speeded up her mobilization, marched light and went into action before fully ready. This accelerated mobilization caught the German army in East Prussia unawares and the Russians were able to claim some early successes. The Germans responded by detaching two army corps from the Western front and replacing the local commander by Hindenburg and Ludendorff who, by swift manoeuvres, destroyed Samsonov's Second Russian Army at Tannenberg and repulsed Rennenkampf's First Army at the battle of the Masurian lakes. Pressure on East Prussia was relieved but the German army in the west had been weakened at a critical moment. To the south, a Russian army group of four armies under Ivanov faced three Austrian armies under the Archduke Frederick and Marshal Conrad. After a month of fierce fighting, the Austrians had been forced back all along the front and had lost their Eastern Polish territories.

By early 1915, the Russian army was posing such a threat to the Central Powers that more German formations had to be transferred from the west. Two offensives were planned, by Hindenburg in East Prussia and by the Austrians in the south against Lemburg. In the north, the Tenth Russian Army was virtually destroyed but the newly formed Twelfth Army held the Germans after an advance of some sixty miles. The Austrian offensive ground to a halt in the Carpathian mountains. The Central Powers now opted instead for a single offensive in Northern Carpathia which met with greater success. The Russian Third Army collapsed and all along the front the Russians were forced back. Lemburg, Lublin and then Warsaw fell. In September, Brest Litovsk was taken and gains of up to 300 miles were achieved with the loss of over 300,000 Russian troops.

In September, Nicholas took over supreme command and Grand-Duke Nicholas was sent to the Caucasus as Viceroy. The Tsar took as his chief-of-staff Alexeiev, a competent strategist and staff officer, but no more than that. Despite the defeats of 1915, Nicholas had every intention of fulfilling his pledge to the French to go on the offensive and began to plan for 1916. The first, in March, around Lake Naroch failed. In May-June however, Brusilov's army group attacking around the valley of the Dniester tore a wide gap in the Austrian armies. Further north, the Russians were unable to make any impression on the German formations facing them. Brusilov continued to make gains into the autumn, having advanced up to 100 miles in places, retaking Warsaw and capturing 400,000 enemy prisoners. The Russian armies had so far held their own but at considerable cost both at the front and at home. Hardship and lack of real success were again feeding the fires of revolution and Nicholas II who had made the fatal mistake of remaining at army headquarters rather than in St Petersburg, failed to read the warning signs. In March 1917, a provisional government was set up under Kerensky and Nicholas was forced to abdicate. But even under her new leadership, Russia still honoured her obligations to the allies and Brusilov launched a further offensive in July. He had some initial success, but with increasing chaos and revolution at home, demoralization set in and the soldiers began to stream home. In November, the Bolsheviks seized power and at once sued for peace.

In its last campaign the Imperial Russian army had been true to its great traditions. It had won great victories and shown resilience in recovering from severe defeats. It had shouldered a massive burden, facing on all fronts as many enemy divisions as the Western powers and had time and time again adapted its plans to support the allies. Final defeat and disintegration came from within. When twenty-five years later the army of the new Soviet state faced the same enemy and as great a crisis as any faced by its predecessors, it was the revival of the traditions and embellishments of the old Imperial army which played such a part in turning the tide and achieving ultimate success.

The Colour Plates

1. Moscow *strelzi*,
    soldier.

2. Moscow strelzi,
    golova.

3. Moscow *strelzi*,
    soldier.

4. L-G Preobrajenski
   Regiment, fusilier.

6. L-G Semenovski
   Regiment, fusilier.

5. L-G Preobrajenski
   Regiment, colonel.

7.   Army Dragoon,
      dragoon.

8.   Artillery Regiment,
      bombardier.

Peter the Great 1686–1725

9. Kiev Infantry
    Regiment, fusilier.

11. Ukrainian cossack.

10. Line infantry, officer.

13. 1st Cuirassier
    Regiment, cuirassier.

12. L-G Ismailovski
    Regiment, fusilier.

14. Line infantry,
    grenadier.

15. L-G Horse Regiment,
    officer.

16. 1st Cadet Corps,
    mounted cadet.

17. Life Company Soldier.

18. General Officer.

19. Life Company Unteroffizier.

20. Army Dragoons,
    dragoon.

21. Grenadier Regiment,
    officer.

Peter III 1761–1762

22. Regiment von
Manteufel, Grenadier
artisan.

24. Regiment von
Manteufel, subaltern.

23. L-G Preobrajenski
Regiment, Colonel.

Peter III 1761–1762

25. Hussar Regiment von
    Zobeltitz, officer.

26. Holstein Life Dragoon
    Regiment, drummer.

27. Army Infantry,
Grenadier.

28. Lieutenant General of
Artillery.

29. Cavalier Guard,
unteroffizier.

30. Line Infantry,
    musketeer.

32. Jaeger Battalion,
    unteroffizier

31. Artilley Regiment,
    soldier.

33. Line infantry,
    drummer.

34. Line infantry,
    subaltern.

35. Line infantry,
    grenadier.

Catherine the Great 1762–1796
Potemkin Corps 1786–1796

36. Light Horse Regiment,
    private.

37. Mounted Rifle
    Regiment, private.

38. L-G Preobrajenski
    Regiment, grenadier.

40. L-G Semenovski,
    Regiment, *unteroffizier*.

39. L-G Ismailovski
    Regiment, subaltern.

Paul I 1796–1801
Guard Cavalry

41. Cavalier Guard
     Regiment, guardsman.

42. Nijegorodski Dragoon
     Regiment,
     Fahnenjunker.

43. Horse Artillery,
bombardier.

44. Malorossiiski
Grenadiers, subaltern.

45. Pavlovski Grenadiers,
fusilier.

46. L-G Ural Cossack
    Sotnia, cossack.

48. Life Hussar Regiment,
    unteroffizier.

47. Field Marshal.

49.　St Petersburg
　　　Grenadier Regiment,
　　　grenadier.

50.　Nevski Musketeer
　　　Regiment, subaltern.

51.　Foot Artillery,
　　　bombardier.

52.   Ahtyrski Hussar
      Regiment, hussar.

54.   Polski Lancer
      Regiment, subaltern.

53.   Orenburg Cossacks,
      officer.

Alexander I 1801–1825
Guards, 1813

56   Cavalier Guard
      Regiment, private.

55   L-G Pavlovski
      Regiment, grenadier.

Alexander I 1801–1825
1809–1813, infantry

57.   Nizovski Musketeer
      Regiment, private.

59.   1st Jaegerski
      Regiment, private.

58.   L-G Jaegerski
      Regiment, subaltern.

60. L-G Hussar
Regiment, *Rotmistre*.

62. Ekaterinoslavski
Cuirassier Regiment,
subaltern.

61. Field-Marshal.

Alexander I 1801–1825
War of 1812

63.   Don Cossacks,
      cossack.

64.   Moscow *Opolchenie,*
      private.

65. L-G Litovski
Regiment,
musician.

66. Cavalier Guard
Regiment, general
officer.

67. L-G Dragoon
Regiment, dragoon.

Alexander I 1801–1825
1817 uniform changes, infantry

68. Keksholmski
    Grenadier Regiment,
    unteroffizier.

69. Grenadier Regiment,
    subaltern.

70. Pioneer battalion,
    sapper.

Nicholas I 1825–1855

71. Palace Grenadiers,
    private.

72. General officer.

73. L-G Preobrajenski
    Regiment, private.

75. L-G Grodno Hussar
Regiment, subaltern.

74. Kimbourg Dragoon
Regiment, dragoon.

76. Cavalier Guard
Regiment, subaltern.

77. Don Cossack Horse
Artillery of the Guard.
General officer.

78. L-G Finlandski
     Regiment, private.

80. Foot Artillery, private.

79. Army Grenadier
     Regiment, officer.

Nicholas I 1825–1855
1844 uniform changes, winter order

81.   Volinski Lancer
        Regiment, lancer.

83.   Smolenski Infantry
        Regiment, soldier.

82.   L-G Horse Regiment,
        officer.

Nicholas I 1825–1855
Caucasian Corps 1848–1855

84. Nijegorodski
Dragoon Regiment,
dragoon.

85. Nijegorodski
Dragoon Regiment,
officer.

86. Infantry, unteroffizier.

87. Grenadier
Regiment,
private.

88. Grenadier Regiment,
officer.

89. Caucasian Corps
Artillery, gunner.

90.   Siberian Lancer
      Regiment, lancer.

91.   Ingermanlandski
      Hussar Regiment,
      hussar.

92.   Minski Infantry
          Regiment, private.

94.   Jakutski Infantry
          Regiment, private.

93.   Tarutinski Jaeger
          Regiment, Captain.

95. Don Cossack Horse
Artillery, gunner.

96. 53rd Don Cossack
Regiment, cossack.

Alexander II 1855–1881
Guards

97. L-G Preobrajenski
     Regiment, private.

98. L-G Horse Grenadier
     Regiment, subaltern.

99.   Life Dragoon
      Pskovski Regiment,
      dragoon.

100.   2nd Life-Hussar
       Pavlovgradski
       Regiment, field
       officer.

101. Orenburgski Line
Battalion, private.

102. Line Infantry,
subaltern.

103. Life Grenadier
Ekaterinoslavski
Regiment, *feldwebel.*

Alexander II 1855–1881
Turkestan 1860–1881

104. Line Battalion,
       private.

105. Orenburg Cossacks,
       cossack.

106. Line Infantry,
       subaltern.

Alexander II 1855–1881
Russo-Turkish War 1877–1878

107. Don Cossacks,
cossack.

108. Nijegorodski
Dragoon Regiment,
officer.

Alexander II 1855–1881
Russo-Turkish War 1877–1878

109.   Line Infantry, soldier.

110.   Line Infantry,
       subaltern.

111.   Line Infantry,
       drummer.

112. Army Artillery,
     private.

114.   Line infantry, private.

113.   Line Infantry,
       subaltern.

Alexander II 1855–1881
Russo-Turkish War 1877–1878

115.   Ľ-G Lancer
       Regiment, gefreiter.

116.   General officer.

117.   L-G Preobrajenski
       Regiment, subaltern.

Alexander III 1881–1894
Guard

118.   L-G Preobrajenski
Regiment, private.

119.   L-G Hussar
Regiment, private.

Alexander III 1881–1894
Cavalry

120. Army Dragoons,
wahmistr.

122. Army Dragoons,
gefreiter.

121. L-G Dragoon
Regiment, field
officer.

123. Line Infantry,
     unteroffizier.

124. Line infantry,
     subaltern.

125. Line infantry, private.

Nicholas II 1894–1917
Russo-Japanese War 1904–1905

126. Line Infantry,
subaltern.

128. Line infantry, private.

127. General officer.

129. Siberian Rifles,
      private.

130. Siberian Rifles,
      officer.

131. Don Cossacks,
      cossack.

Nicholas II 1894–1917
Uniform changes 1906, guard infantry

132.   L-G Preobrajenski
       Regiment, private.

134.   L-G Litovski
       Regiment, *feldwebel*.

133.   L-G Ismailovski
       Regiment, subaltern.

Nicholas II 1894–1917
Uniform changes, 1906, guard cavalry

135. L-G Hussar
Regiment,
unteroffizier.

136. Cavalier Guard
Regiment, officer.

137. L-G Lancer
Regiment, officer.

Nicholas II 1894–1917
Parade uniforms 1909–1917

138. L-G Jaegerski
Regiment, Colonel.

139. L-G Hussar
Regiment, general
officer.

140. General Staff, field
officer.

141. L-G Imperial Family
     Rifle Battalion,
     unteroffizier.

142. Cavalier Guard
     Regiment, private.

143. L-G 1st Artillery
     Brigade, *unteroffizier*.

Nicholas II 1894–1917
Parade uniforms 1909–1917,
army cavalry

144. 10th Lancers Odessa
      Regiment, lancer.

145. 13th Dragoon
      Regiment, subaltern.

Nicholas II 1894–1917
Parade uniforms, 1909–1917, cossacks

146. L-G Cossack
Regiment,
unteroffizier.

147. L-G Atamanski
Regiment, field
officer.

148. His Imperial
Majesty's Own
Convoy, cossack.

149.   Army Artillery, officer.

150.   General officer.

151.   General officer.

152. Line Infantry,
     private.

154. Aviation Service,
     subaltern.

153. L-G Preobrajenski
     Regiment, subaltern.

155. 5th Hussar
Regiment, hussar.

156. Army Artillery,
Lieut.-Colonel.

157. Army Infantry,
private.

158. Don Cossacks,
officer.

159. Automobile unit,
private.

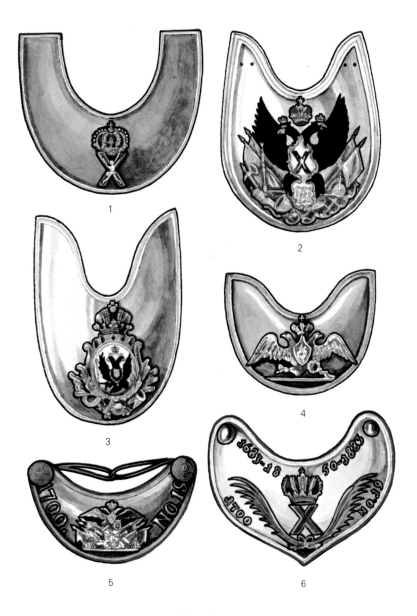

1

2

3

4

5

6

160   Gorgets

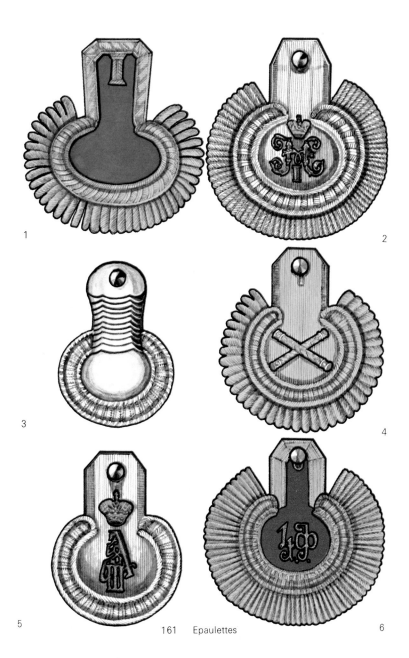

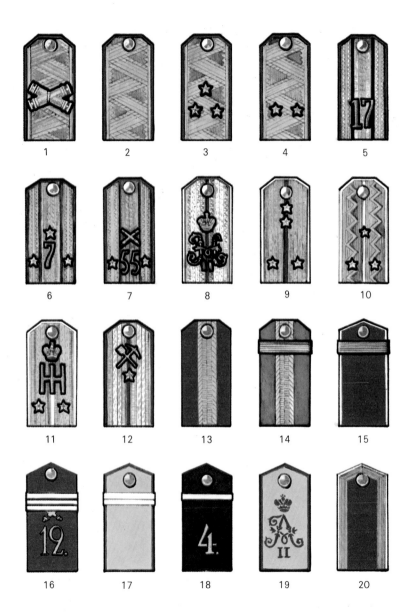

1   2   3   4   5

6   7   8   9   10

11   12   13   14   15

16   17   18   19   20

162   *Pogoni* (shoulder boards)

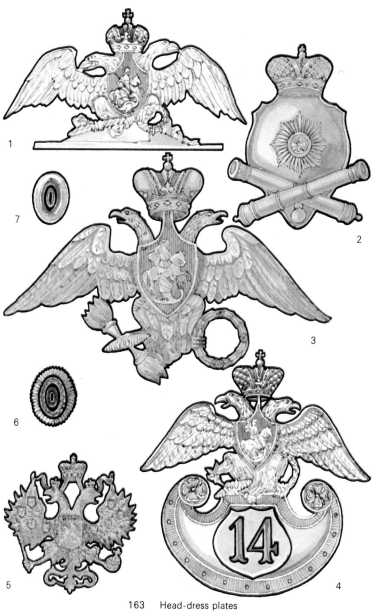

163   Head-dress plates

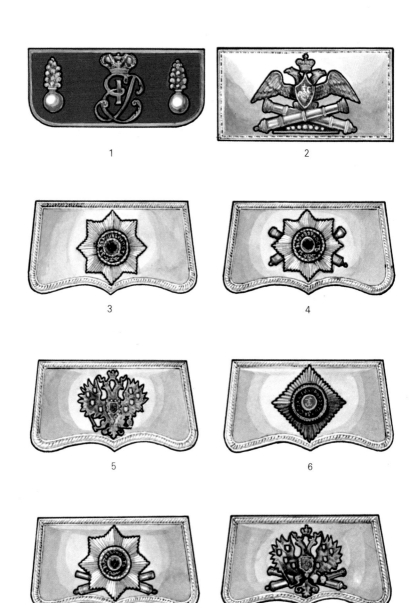

1

2

3

4

5

6

7

8

164   Pouches

Plate Descriptions

Plate 1
Peter the Great, 1686–1725.
Moscow *strelzi*, late seventeenth century.

The *strelzi* formed regiments and garrisons in large towns and fortresses and acted as gendarmerie for the maintenance of law and order. They were abolished by Peter in 1698 after rising against him while on a tour abroad, many of them suffering execution or imprisonment, others being absorbed into the new regiments being formed by Peter.

1 10th Moscow, Theodor Lopoukin, Regiment. Soldier.
The uniform of the *strelzi* was issued by the state and colours and style were regulated. This soldier wears the crimson cap, yellow *kaftan* and green boots distinctive to his regiment. His armament includes a matchlock musket, a bandolier with powder charges, a sabre and a *berdysh*, a battle-axe which doubled as a musket rest.

2 1st Moscow, Igor Loutokhin, Regiment. *Golova* or captain.
Officers of *strelzi* conformed to the general details of uniform of the soldiers but wore garments of higher quality. His hat is fur-lined and ornamented and embroidered in gold. He carries a sabre and his staff of office.

3 7th Moscow, Stepan Ivanov, Regiment. Soldier.
He wears his regimental uniform of a light blue *kaftan* with black loops, crimson cap and yellow boots.

Plate 2
Peter the Great, 1686–1725
Guard Regiments, 1700–1720

4 L-G Preobrajenski Regiment. Fusilier.
The senior regiment of the new regular Russian army, nominally dating from 1683 when Tsarevitch Peter, then aged only eleven was allowed to form his own regiment from his *poteshni* or playmates. Strictly speaking however they were not incorporated into the army as a regiment until some time later. In 1700 the regiment was given the title Life-Guard Preobrajenski Regiment after the crown estate where Peter spent his childhood, and later the same year, the regiment greatly distinguished itself at the battle of Narva. The regiment wore a western-style uniform including the dark green coats which were to become standard dress for the army as a whole.

5 L-G Preobrajenski Regiment. Colonel.

The first Colonel of the L-G Preobrajenski Regiment was Tsar Peter
himself and thereafter it became the
rule for every Russian monarch to
assume this office. The Tsar is shown
in regimental uniform with his
Colonel's gorget which is still pre-
served in the Hermitage Museum.
He wears also the star and sash of the
Order of St Andrew, Russia's premier order instituted by himself and
an officer's sash of white, blue and red
silk, the national colours of Imperial
Russia.

6 L-G Semenovski Regiment. Fusilier.

The second Russian guard regiment
which also began as a *poteshni* regiment and was named after another
crown estate. Its original regimental
colour was blue (perhaps because of
the shortage of green cloth at the
time) but in 1720 the regiment was
given dark green coats with blue
collar and cuffs, a combination retained into modern times.

Plate 3
Peter the Great, 1686–1725.
Cavalry, artillery, 1700–1720.

7 Army Dragoon Regiment. Dragoon.

Peter attached great importance to
dragoons in their traditional role of
fighting both mounted and on foot,
and by the end of his reign there
were thirty-three dragoon regiments.
They were dressed and equipped
much like infantry with the addition

of *botforti* or heavy boots when in the
mounted role. Their armament
varied and included muskets or car-
bines, sabres or *pallashes* and pistols.

8 Artillery Regiment. Bombardier.

The one artillery regiment which
existed under Peter was divided into
one bombardier company, six cannon
companies, one miner company and
smaller commands of engineers and
pontoons. The bombardier company
shown here was equipped with hand
mortars or *mortirka*. Their uniform
colour varied but when possible it
consisted of red coats with blue cuffs,
red trousers, blue cloaks and white or
striped stockings.

Plate 4
Peter the Great, 1686–1725.
Infantry, Cossacks, 1700–1725.

9 Kiev Infantry Regiment. Fusilier.

Although it was decreed that the
uniforms of line infantry should be
the same as those of the guard, there
was no certainty of supply of cloth of
a particular colour and Colonels
dressed their regiments in whatever
cloth was available, more often than
not the local undyed variety which
came out in various shades of grey.
In other respects, the Russian in-
fantryman now looked very much
like his counterpart in the armies of
Western Europe.

10 Line Infantry. Officer.

Line infantry officers too were supposed to wear the same uniform as

officers of guard infantry but, like the soldiers, used any cloth that was available. Their officer status was indicated by the sash in the national colours of white, red and blue and by the halberd.

11 Ukrainian Cossack.

Following the takeover of Ukraine by Russia from Poland, the Ukrainian cossacks transferred their allegiance to the Russian crown. Like the Don cossacks they formed their own separate *voysko* headed by their own *hetmen* and retained their national dress of *kaftan*, baggy *sharovary* (trousers) and boots, all of which were of any chosen colours. Their armament included curved Turkish sabres and muskets of a variety of patterns.

Plate 5
Anna Ioannovna, 1730–1740.

Following the recommendations of the military commission set up by the Empress, a third guard infantry regiment named the Life-Guard Ismailovski Regiment (after another crown estate) was formed and the Leib Dragoon Regiment was converted to cuirassiers, given guard status and called the Life-Guard Horse Regiment.

12 L-G Ismailovski Regiment. Fusilier.

Under Anne, the uniform of guard and line infantry regiments remained basically unchanged, consisting of dark green *kaftan* with red collar and cuffs. Waistcoat, trousers and cloak were also red and instead of stockings, white gaiters were now worn. The difference between guard and line regiments was that the former wore double-headed eagles on their cartridge pouches while the latter had newly introduced regimental badges. The Life-Guard Ismailovski Regiment had dark-green collars which they retained into modern times.

13 1st Cuirassier, Münnich Regiment. Cuirassier.

In 1731 the Viborgski Dragoon Regiment was renamed the 1st Cuirassier Münnich Regiment and later two other dragoon regiments were converted into cuirassiers. The cuirassiers' uniform was for general wear much like that of dragoons and for parade wear, a natural-coloured elkskin *collet*, waistcoat and breeches. Both *collet* and waistcoat were lined with red cloth. Over the *collet* was worn an iron cuirass with the brass cypher of the Empress and the Imperial crown. The armament comprised a *palash*, carbine and a pair of pistols.

Plate 6
Anna Ioannovna, 1730–1740.

Under Field Marshal Münnich began the Prussian influence in the Russian army. Uniforms became tighter, much to the discomfort of the peasant soldier accustomed to loose clothing. The curling, powdering and plaiting of hair, equally hated, had to be tolerated for over sixty years.

14 Line Infantry Regiment. Grenadier.

The uniform of the grenadier differed from that of the fusilier only in the tall cloth *grenadierka* or mitre cap, with green top, red band and brass plate on the front bearing the regimental crest and in the brass matchholder on the pouch-belt.

15 Life-Guard Horse Regiment. Officer in everyday dress.

The Life-Guard Horse Regiment was the first, and at that time, the only guard cavalry regiment as the Cavalier-Guards were called together from other units only for special ceremonial occasions and were dispersed after the event. The uniform of the L-G Horse Regiment was similar to that of other cuirassier regiments but was more elaborate in some respects. Officers had their *collets* and waistcoats richly trimmed in gold lace and their cuirasses were brightly polished and trimmed in blue. This officer is shown in the everyday dress of cornflower blue coat and red waistcoat and trousers.

16 1st Cadet Corps. Cadet on mounted duties.

The 1st Cadet Corps was instituted in 1731 to provide a military and general education for the sons of the nobility. The Corps had infantry and cavalry sections which wore uniforms similar to, but richer than, the corresponding army units. In this case the cadet on mounted duties wears an elkskin supervest embellished with a black double-headed eagle and trimmed in red cloth.

Plate 7
Elizabeth Petrovna, 1741–1761.

17 The Life Company, 1742. Soldier in Cavalier-Guard order.

The principal part in the coup d'état which brought Elizabeth to the throne was played by the Grenadier Company of the L-G Preobrajenski Regiment. In recognition, the company was separated from the regiment and was reformed into a special privileged unit under the title 'Life-Company'. Every soldier was ennobled and was considered equal in rank to an officer of the army. At the coronation of Elizabeth and on other ceremonial occasions, the Company acted as Cavalier Guards and wore the corresponding uniform. On other occasions the uniform was basically the same as before but finer in quality and with many embellishments of officer quality.

18 General officer, 1756. Field Marshal Count Apraksin.

In October 1756, Count Apraksin was appointed commander-in-chief of the Russian army in the field. Although he had had a distinguished military career, he had had little experience of commanding a large army at war, particularly against such an adversary as Frederick the Great of Prussia. In his first battle at Gross Jägersdorf in the summer of 1757, he was successful but he failed to exploit his victory by decisive action and was recalled and court-martialled. Though acquitted, he died of a stroke.

19   The Life Company, 1741–61. *Unteroffizier* in parade order.

A sergeant in the Life-Company was equivalent to a Captain in the army. The uniform, of officer quality, comprised a green *kaftan* with red collar and cuffs, richly laced with gold and gold epaulettes. Caps were richly decorated with gold lace and ostrich feathers, reminiscent of the theatrical masque beloved of the eighteenth century court. He is armed with an officer's court sword and fusil.

Plate 8
Seven Years War, 1756–1762.

20   Army Dragoons, 1756–1762. Dragoon.

At this period there were twenty-nine dragoon regiments each comprising ten dragoon and two horse grenadier companies and in addition, each regiment had two 3-pounder and four 6-pounder mortars attached. Their uniform remained unchanged except that cloaks were red instead of cornflower blue. Dragoons were armed with the straight heavy cavalry *palash* and musket with bayonet.

21   Army Grenadier Regiment 1756–1762. Officer.

In 1756 the grenadier companies of the third battalion of every infantry regiment were brought together to form four grenadier regiments. The uniform of a grenadier officer was the same as that of a fusilier except for the grenadier cap which had a gilt plate with the royal cypher rather than the regimental badge. The officer's sash was now in the colours of the Order of St George, black and gold for field officers, black and yellow for subalterns.

Plate 9
Peter III, 1761–1762.

In 1742 the nephew of Elizabeth Petrovna, the fourteen-year-old Karl-Ulrich, Herzog von Holstein Gottorp was declared heir to the Russian throne, converted to Orthodoxy and renamed Peter. He remained the ruling Herzog von Holstein and as such, brought with him, a detachment of Holstein troops. When, in 1761, he ascended the Russian throne as Peter III, he ended the war with Prussia and immediately began to reorganize the Russian army in the Prussian manner, much to the displeasure of officers and soldiers.

22   Musketeer Regiment Zege von Manteufel. Grenadier Artisan.

The Holstein Corps in Russia included eight musketeer regiments, numerically smaller than their Russian counterparts. Their uniform comprised blue coat with red collar and cuffs, white waistcoats and white trousers. Grenadiers wore Prussian-style caps with the combined arms of Russia and Holstein and with the cypher 'P', but without the number

'III' as Peter was the first Holstein ruler to bear that name.

23 Life-Guard Preobrajenski Regiment. Colonel. Tsar Peter III.

In accordance with the established tradition, Peter assumed the Colonelcy of the L-G Preobrajenski Regiment on ascending the throne, and he was painted in regimental uniform during his brief reign. He wears a gorget of the same pattern as the previous reign but with his own cypher added. The Prussian influence is apparent in the style and cut of his uniform.

24 Musketeer Regiment Zege von Manteufel. Subaltern.

The officer's spontoon and gorget both bore Peter's cypher without the number 'III'. His coat was richly embroidered with gold, the expense of which was a further cause of discontent among the poorly paid officers.

Plate 10
Peter III, 1761–1762.

25 Hussar Regiment von Zobeltitz. Officer.

The Holstein cavalry in Russia included seven regiments of which two were hussars. Their uniforms were of the Prussian style with conical caps or *mirletons* and with the cypher 'P' on holsters, sabretache and shabraque.

26 Holstein Life-Dragoon Regiment. Drummer.

The senior Holstein cavalry regiment was the Life-Dragoon Regiment

which had guard status. Dragoon drummers of this period carried infantry-style drums which could be used mounted or dismounted as well as kettle drums; drummers were distinguished by their wings and braided sleeves. The Holstein units took no part in the coup d'état which ended in the imprisonment and death of Peter. They returned peacefully to their homeland and had no further links with the Russian army.

Plate 11
Catherine the Great, 1762–1796.

On her accession to the throne, Catherine began by abolishing all the innovations of her husband, Peter III, and restored the army to the state of the reign of Elizabeth Petrovna. She then instituted a military commission to review the state of the armed forces in the light of experience gained during the Seven Years War. In due course the commission recommended the restoration of a number of Peter's innovations.

27 Army Infantry, Grenadier Company 1763. Private.

In January 1763 it was decreed that there should be forty-six infantry regiments, of which four were to be grenadier regiments. Each regiment consisted of two battalions and an artillery command and each battalion included one grenadier and five musketeer companies. The Prussian-style grenadier cap introduced by Peter III was retained.

28 Lieutenant-General of Artillery. Count Melissino (1726–1797).

The Regulations of 1764 for the first time laid down a uniform for general officers to consist of green *kaftans*, red waistcoats and red trousers. The Lieutenant-General was distinguished by one narrow and one broad band of laurel leaf embroidery on coat, cuffs and pockets. After distinguished service in the Seven Years War and Turkish Wars, Melissino was made Director of the Artillery and Engineering Cadet Corps. He was later appointed Inspector of Artillery. He therefore wears the red *kaftan* and black facings of artillery rather than the green uniform.

29 Cavalier Guard 1763. Under-officer.

In 1764, the Life-Company of the Preobrajenski Regiment were formed into a Cavalier Guards Corps of sixty specially selected officers who were given nominal ranks of junior officers and senior NCOs. They were clothed in spectacular if not theatrical uniforms for their ceremonial duties.

Plate 12
Catherine the Great, 1762–1796.

30 Line Infantry 1763. Musketeer.

The uniform of the infantry remained basically the same as during the reign of Elizabeth Petrovna but some features introduced by Peter III were retained, notably the coat lapels.

31 Artillery Regiment 1763. Soldier.

At first the artillery retained their traditional red uniforms although later, these were altered to green with black facings. Over the right shoulder was worn a buff belt and powder flask with two primer pins attached to the belt. There were five artillery regiments in addition to the artillery commands of infantry regiments.

32 Jaeger Battalion 1777–1786. *Unteroffizier.*

In 1765, Light Infantry or Jaeger commands of sixty men were formed in some infantry regiments and in 1769, the system was extended to all infantry regiments. In 1777, the Jaeger commands were formed into separate battalions and in 1785 into Jaeger Corps of four battalions each. They were given different uniforms from normal infantry including black felt caps, short jackets and trousers and boots in place of gaiters. They were armed with short muskets and flat bayonets. It was, in all, a remarkably modern concept of uniform.

Plate 13
Catherine the Great, 1762–1796.
Potemkin Corps, 1786–1796.

In April 1786, Catherine approved new uniforms based on the ideas of Prince Potemkin-Tavrichesky which were revolutionary for his period, 'the beauty and purpose of military uniform is its correspondence to its use', 'to curl and powder hair, is it the soldier's business' and 'is it not more appropriate to wash hair than mess it with grease'.

33 Line Infantry, Potemkin Corps, 1786. Drummer.

The main features of the Potemkin uniform were the unusual helmet of felt and leather with transverse woollen crest, short *kurtka* and sleeveless waistcoat, long wide overalls with leather reinforcements to the lower parts worn over short soft boots.

34 Line Infantry, Potemkin Corps, 1788. Subaltern officer in service dress.

In 1788 the use of the new uniforms was extended to officers of line regiments to be worn when on duty. His officer status is indicated by the 1788 pattern gorget and he also carries an officer's lightweight fusil and half sabre. Unlike other ranks, officers continued to powder their hair and retained their plaits.

35 Line Infantry, Potemkin Corps, 1786. Grenadier

Equipment of the infantry soldier included a leather waistbelt, cartouche pouch and belt, leather pack and waterbottle. Summer uniform consisted of a white linen *kitel* of the same pattern as the *kurtka* and linen trousers without the leather reinforcement.

**Plate 14
Catherine the Great, 1762–1796.
Potemkin Corps, 1786–1796.**

36 Light Horse Regiment 1786. Private.

In 1786, hussar regiments were converted to Light Horse and were given a uniform similar to that of the in-

fantry comprising blue *kurtkas* with red collars, cuffs and facings, red trousers with leather reinforcement and helmets with white crests. In addition there was a white aiguillette attached to the right shoulder.

37 Mounted Rifle Regiment, 1786. Private.

In February 1788, mounted rifle commands of light horse regiments were given dark green *kurtkas* and trousers. Their leather equipment was black instead of white and their helmets had green crests. In 1789, Potemkin formed mounted rifle regiments which wore hussar *mirletons* instead of the transverse-crested helmets.

**Plate 15
Paul I, 1796–1801.
Guard Infantry.**

During the reign of his mother, Catherine, Paul had been allowed to form a miniature army at his residence *Gatchina* which included infantry, cavalry, artillery and even naval forces and he modelled them on the armies of Frederick the Great and of his father, Peter III. On his accession, he introduced this style for the army as a whole much to the discomfort of officers and soldiers accustomed to Potemkin-style uniforms.

38 Life-Guard Preobrajenski Regiment, 1797–1801. Grenadier.

In 1797 guard infantry were given green *kaftans*, white waistcoats and trousers, and high gaiters, white for parade and black for other orders of dress. The L-G Preobrajenski Regiment had red collars and cuffs. Grenadiers were given new Prussian style mitre caps with gilt plates and red cloth *kolpaks*.

39 Life-Guard Ismailovski Regiment, 1797–1801. Subaltern officer.

The Ismailovski Regiment wore dark green collars, a distinction retained into modern times. Cockades of black with orange edging were reintroduced and sashes of silver, black and orange. This combination of colours was becoming used more and more in military appointments although they were never officially acknowledged as national colours.

40 Life-Guard Semenovski Regiment, 1796–1797. Under-officer.

The Semenovski Regiment wore blue collar and cuffs. The NCO's tricorne had a braid edging to the rim and he wears his hair powdered and carries a spontoon in the Prussian style.

Cavalier Guard of his mother. In December 1796 he formed a second squadron and in January 1797, a third. In October 1797, all three were disbanded. In January 1799, having proclaimed himself Grand-Master of the Sovereign Order of St John of Jerusalem, he decided that such an exalted person should have his own Guards and he formed a squadron of Grand-Master's Cavalier Guard. Finally in March 1800, with the addition of two further squadrons, Paul formed the Cavalier Guard Regiment, no longer an elite ceremonial unit called only for special occasions, but a regular Guard Cuirassier Regiment, senior to the L-G Horse Regiment.

42 Nijegorodski Dragoon Regiment 1797. Fahnen-Junker.

Line cavalry under Paul included five regiments of cuirassiers, sixteen carabineer and eleven dragoon regiments. The uniforms of dragoons were still much the same as infantry, but with buff waistcoats and trousers, and riding boots. The cavalry standards introduced by Paul were of Prussian pattern.

Plate 16
Paul I, 1796–1801.
Cavalry.

41 Cavalier Guard Regiment, 1800–1801. Cavalier Guardsman.

On his accession Paul immediately formed his own Cavalier Guard Squadron, ignoring the existing

Plate 17
Paul I, 1796–1801.
Horse Artillery, Infantry.

43 Horse Artillery, 1797. Bombardier.

On his accession, Paul also completely reorganized the artillery which now formed ten field artillery battalions, three siege and one horse. It also had attached, one pioneer regiment and eight pontoon sections. In March 1800 they were reformed into seven artillery regiments and one horse artillery regiment. The uniform of horse artillery was the same as that of foot except for boots in place of gaiters. Armament consisted of dragoon-pattern *palashes* and pistols.

44 Malorossiiski Grenadier Regiment, 1797–1801. Subaltern officer.

The infantry did not escape Paul's mania for reorganization, old regiments were disbanded, new ones formed and all were constantly renamed. At Paul's death there were eighty-one regiments including thirteen grenadier, forty-nine musketeer and nineteen jaeger. The new uniforms of the infantry were officially confirmed by the 'All-Highest Ukase' of 5 January 1798. In grenadier regiments, while the soldiers wore Prussian style mitre caps, officers continued to wear tricornes trimmed in gold, with orange and black cockades. The officer wears also the new standard pattern gorget of Prussian style introduced for all guard and line infantry.

45 Pavlovski Grenadier Regiment, 1796–1801. Fusilier.

The mitre cap with metal plate was smaller for fusiliers than for grenadiers. The Pavlovski Regiment, later one of the most famous of Russian Guard Regiments was formed from other units in 1790 and at this date did not have guard status.

Plate 18
Paul I, 1796–1801.
Italian Campaign, 1799.

46 Life-Guard, Ural Cossack Sotnia, 1799. Cossack.

The expansion of the Russian empire resulted in a great increase in cossacks who were settled in the newly conquered territories. They were obliged to serve the Tsar as long as they were capable of bearing arms and they formed units of irregular cavalry. Their uniforms, weapons and horse equipment were different from the rest of the cavalry and they rode in their own particular style. The L-G Ural Cossack Sotnia was originally part of Paul's Gatchina Corps. In 1798 they were given raspberry coloured *kaftans* trimmed with silver for officers and white for cossacks. They were armed with sabres, pistols and lances (their most formidable weapon).

47 Field Marshal, 1779. Alexander Vassilovitch Souvorov, Prince Italiiski, Count Rymnikski.

Souvorov was the greatest of all Russian military commanders who never lost a battle. In the reign of Catherine, Souvorov fought Turks and Poles. At the beginning of Paul's reign, he disapproved of some of the new Emperor's innovations and was relieved of his commands but was recalled for the Italian Campaign of 1799. He died in 1800. He is shown in a Field Marshal's undress uniform which lacks the heavy gold embroidery of the dress uniform.

48 Life-Hussar Regiment, 1796–1801. Non-commissioned officer.

The Life-Hussar Regiment was formed by Paul from his mother's Life-Hussar Squadron and from his Gatchina hussar and cossack regiments. At first it was known as the 'Life-Hussar Cossack Regiment' but after only a month the hussar and cossack elements were separated.

Plate 19
Alexander I, 1801–1825.
1805 uniform changes, infantry.

On his accession to the throne, Alexander retained many of the changes introduced by his father but immediately abolished some of the more excessive and unpopular changes. He introduced new uniforms of his own design which remained basically unchanged until the middle of the nineteenth century.

49 St Petersburg Grenadier Regiment, 1805. Grenadier.

One of Alexander's first orders was for the abolition of powdered hair and for soldiers to cut their hair short. The new uniform included dark green *mundir* with stand-up collars and cuffs in regimental facing colour, white trousers and short boots. The 1805-pattern *kiver* had a black horsehair plume, black and orange cockade and brass grenade badge.

50 Nevski Musketeer Regiment, 1809. Subaltern officer.

Officers adopted *kivers* in place of bicorn hats in 1809. White linen trousers with buttons for summer wear were introduced in 1807. In 1807 also, officers spontoons and canes were abolished.

51 Foot Artillery, 1806. Bombardier.

The changes introduced for the infantry applied also to foot artillery except that the collars and cuffs of the *mundir* were black with red piping (a feature retained into modern times). Equipment included leather pack, cartouche pouch and infantry hanger.

Plate 20
Alexander I, 1801–1825.
1805 uniform changes, cavalry.

52 Ahtyrski Hussar Regiment, 1803–1809. Hussar.

In general, hussar regiments retained their traditional uniforms with only minor alterations. In 1803, the *mirleton* was replaced by the *kiver*, and double-headed eagles on appointments were replaced by the Tsar's cypher. Uniform colour varied from regiment to regiment and was constantly changed and white trousers were gradually replaced by coloured trousers.

53 Orenburg Cossack Regiment, 1801–1809. Officer.

Alexander I regularized the uniform of cossacks who had hitherto worn more or less what they liked. The basic uniform included blue *chekmen* piped in red, blue overalls and black fur cap with red bag. Officers were dressed in much the same way as the cossacks, but with orange, black and gold feather plumes, and silver, black and gold cap cords. In 1804, officers were given silver embroidery of special design on their collars, later retained only by Life-Guard Cossack regiments.

54 Polski Lancer Regiment, 1807. Subaltern in service order.

In 1803, Alexander converted two light horse regiments into lancers and approved their Polish-style uniforms which became the pattern for lancers of many other armies, particularly the tall square-topped *czapska* and *kurtka* with plastron, in this case omitted in service order.

Plate 21
Alexander I, 1801–1825.
Guard Regiments, 1813.

55 Life-Guard Pavlovski Regiment. Grenadier.

Grenadier mitre caps were abolished in 1805, but the *kivers* which replaced them did not reach the troops until some time later and the Pavlovski Grenadier Regiment still wore their mitres during the 1807 campaign. For their conduct at the Battle of Friedland, Alexander I ordered that the Regiment should retain its cap 'in the state in which they left the battle-field as visible mark of its bravery and Our grace'. In 1813, in commemoration of their services during the 1812 campaign, the Regiment was re-named the L-G Pavlovski Regiment and was incorporated into the Imperial Guard. Over 600 of the caps

originally worn at Friedland were still in use to the end of the Empire.

56 Cavalier Guard Regiment, 1812. Private.

Crested helmets were first issued to cuirassiers in 1803. In 1808, the size of the crest was reduced and in 1812, black cuirasses with red cord edging were issued to all guard and army cuirassiers. The use of the St Andrew's star in place of the double-headed eagle to denote guard regiments dates from this period.

Plate 22
Alexander I, 1801–1825.

57 Nizovski Musketeer Regiment, 1809. Private in winter marching order.

The *shinel* was introduced by Alexander I and soon became very popular among the soldiers who liked nothing better than to leave their tight jackets in store and wear something akin to the comfortable *kaftan* of their fore-fathers. The shako is the 1809 pattern with reinforcing chevrons on the side and a coloured pompom denoting the battalion, in this case red for 3rd Battalion (white for 1st, yellow for 2nd).

58 Life-Guard Jaegerski Regiment, 1813. Subaltern officer in marching order.

He wears the 1812 pattern *kiver* with its distinctively Russian scuttle shape, later also adopted by the Prussian army. His rank is indicated by the epaulettes without fringe and by the leather pack worn only by junior officers. The overalls are buttoned down the side and are leather-reinforced.

59 1st Jaegerski Regiment, 1809. Private in marching order.
The shako is the 1809 pattern. Jaegerski regiments wore the usual infantry jacket, but were distinguished by dark green trousers and black equipment. The *shinel* is worn rolled over the left shoulder.

Plate 23
Alexander I, 1801–1825.
War of 1812.

60 Life-Guard Hussar Regiment, 1813. *Rotmistre* **(cavalry captain) in campaign order. Denis Davidov.**
Ten years of almost uninterrupted campaigning brought many changes in the way uniforms were worn. Officers started wearing the soldier's *furashka* and even Koutousov himself was often depicted wearing one. Gold and silver lace was allowed to be substituted by yellow and white wool. Some partisan leaders discarded uniforms altogether and adopted peasants' attire to match their motley units. Davidov was a poet and a partisan leader in the war against Napoleon.

61 Field Marshal in parade order, 1812. Michael Illarionovitch Koutousov.
He wears the 1812 pattern coatee of his rank with general's epaulettes.

Koutousov lost the sight of his right eye fighting the Turks alongside Souvorov. After the defeat of the Russian army at Austerlitz where he was nominal commander but where the vital decisions were taken by Alexander himself, he was not again given command until Napoleon's invasion of Russia in 1812 and only then when the position became critical. Immensely popular he brought new spirit to the army. As a result of his tactics, his ability of handling both officers and soldiers and above all his choice to sacrifice Moscow rather than lose the army, Napoleon and his Grand Army were defeated. Koutousov died early in 1813.

62 Ekaterinoslavski Cuirassier Regiment, 1812. Subaltern officer in campaign order.
He wears the *furashka* and *surtuk* which served as both frock coat and greatcoat, with fringeless epaulettes. His overalls are reinforced with leather.

Plate 24
Alexander I, 1801–1825.
War of 1812.

63 Don Cossack Voiskoe, 1812. Cossack.
Cossacks played an important role in Russia's struggle against Napoleon. In 1812, the Don cossacks alone provided over 40,000 fully equipped and trained men and they not only performed their usual roles of reconnaissance, escort, rounding up of enemy stragglers and foragers but

also took an active part in major battles in massed cavalry actions. Their contribution to the destruction of the Grand Army was particularly great during the retreat from Moscow when the French were surrounded by masses of cossacks and harassed by them day and night.

64 Moscow Opolchenie 1812–1814. Private.

The *Opolchenie* were raised by the 'All-Highest Ukase' of 15 July 1812. Each province was responsible for assembling, clothing and arming a specified number of soldiers, mainly from the local peasantry. Officers were chosen from civil servants, retired officers or young landed gentry. Both clothing and equipment varied a great deal from fancy and opulence to slightly militarized peasant's attire. All however had to have the *opolchenie* cross and royal cypher on their hats.

Plate 25
Alexander I, 1801–1825.
1817 uniform changes.

65 Life-Guard Litovski Regiment, 1818. Musician in summer marching order.

The L-G Litovski Regiment was formed in 1811 and formed together with the L-G Ismailovski Regiment the 2nd Brigade of the Guard Infantry Division. After a later reorganization, it became the 1st Regiment of the 3rd Guard Infantry Division. The *kiver* is of the pattern introduced in 1817, and in 1818, after the Regi-

ment's attachment to the Lithuanian Corps, it was given yellow collar, cuffs and plastron. The *kiver* plate and buttons of the Regiment bore the double-headed eagle with the Lithuanian crest of the rider on the central shield in place of the usual image of St George.

66 Cavalier Guard Regiment, 1825. General in *vice-mundir* Tsar Alexander I.

This simple yet formal uniform typifies Alexander's character at the latter end of his reign. After the defeat of Napoleon and his triumphal entry into Paris, Alexander returned a changed man. He became deeply religious and reverted to the stricter discipline of his childhood at Gatchino. The wearing of medals on a bar was a Russian innovation and Alexander's medals are the Order of St George, 4th Class, medal of 1812, Austrian Order of Maria Theresa, Prussian Iron Cross, Dutch Order of Wilhelm and the Prussian 1813–14 medals. The star is the Order of St Andrew combined with a Garter and the Swedish Order of the Sword.

67 Life-Guard Dragoon Regiment 1817. Dragoon.

In 1817, dragoon regiments, both guard and army reverted to their traditional mounted infantry uniforms with *kivers*, *mundirs* and long leather reinforced trousers in place of crested helmets and white breeches. Guard regiments were given coloured lapels to their *mundirs*, which after the introduction of tunics, were replaced by button-on plastrons, a feature of Russian ceremonial uniform to recent times.

Plate 26
Alexander I, 1801–1825.
1817 uniform changes.

68   Keksholmski Grenadier
Regiment, 1817.
***Unteroffizier* in marching**
order.
The influence of contact with other
armies during the Napoleonic Wars
is apparent. The *kiver* and black
buttoned gaiters have a distinctively
French appearance and the *kiver*
plate, adopted for all except guard
regiments was taken from the British
1812–16 pattern.

69   Grenadier Regiment, 1817.
Subaltern officer in parade
order.
Above the *kiver* plate is an amazon
shield with the inscription '*Sa Otlichie*'
('for distinction'). The shield was
later replaced by metal ribbons or
scrolls. The gorget is of the smaller
pattern introduced in 1808.

70   Pioneer Battalion, 1817.
Sapper in marching order.
The uniform of the pioneers was
much the same as that of the artillery
with the exception that they had
white *pribor* instead of yellow. Every
man carried spades or other equipment in leather holders.

Plate 27
Nicholas I, 1825–1855.
General Staff and Guard.

71   Palace Grenadiers, 1827.
Private.
Following the participation of some
guard units in the Decembrists' up-

rising, Nicholas I was uncertain how
far he could trust his immediate
guard. He therefore formed in 1827 a
special Company of Palace Grenadiers with all ranks, including the
officers, selected from NCOs with
long and unblemished service. Their
uniforms were quite unlike those of
any other Russian unit. The bearskin
cap was taken from the French (and
at first captured French caps were
used with the plates changed) and
the laced jackets were similar to those
worn by the Prussian Schloss-
Grenadiers.

72   General Officer c.1830.
The aiguillette and cypher on the
epaulettes denote that he is a general
adjutant to the Tsar. The bottom
button of the cuff is undone, an
affectation dating from the early
years of Alexander I's reign when
sleeves were cut very tight and which
was carried on into modern times.

73   Life-Guard Preobajenski
Regiment, c.1830. Private
in summer parade order.
The uniform of guard infantry
changed little during the reign of
Nicholas I and the only difference
between this figure and that of the
earlier reign is the change from overalls to trousers and the wearing of
gaiters under the trousers which
lasted only a short while.

Plate 28
Nicholas I, 1825–1855.
Cavalry to 1844.

74   Kimbourg Dragoon
Regiment No. 3. Private.
The only change from the uniform of

the previous reign was the replacement of the English-style *kiver* plate for infantry, dragoons and hussars, by a double-headed eagle plate of army pattern.

75 Life-Guard Grodno Hussar Regiment, 1825–1831. Subaltern officer in parade order.

The *kiver* plate is the guard pattern, a larger double-headed eagle without the shield below. The Regiment was formed in 1824 at Seidlitz in Poland and was recruited from Poles already serving in other units. The Regiment was awarded old guard status for its part in the suppression of the Polish uprising in 1831, after which its uniform was changed because it was considered too Polish in its colours.

Plate 29
Nicholas I, 1825–1855.
1844 uniform changes.

76 Cavalier Guard Regiment, 1844. Subaltern officer in parade order.

The famous and distinctive guard cuirassier helmet surmounted with the double-headed eagle first appeared in 1844 when the crests of the existing leather helmets were removed and replaced by the eagle. Later in the same year, new metal helmets with lobster tails based on the Prussian style were introduced. At the same time, the black cuirasses were replaced by yellow metal.

77 Don Cossack Horse Artillery of the Guard. General Officer. Tsar Nicholas I.

As Tsar, Nicholas was automatically Colonel-in-Chief of several guard units. Before becoming Tsar he had commanded the Guard Sapper Battalion and the 1st Guard Infantry Division. The Guard Horse Artillery Brigade of six batteries included one battery of Don Cossack Horse Artillery which wore distinctive fur caps and the long *mundir* peculiar to the cossacks.

Plate 30
Nicholas I, 1825–1855.
1844 Uniform Changes.

78 Life-Guard Finlandski Regiment. Private in summer parade order.

The leather 'pickelhaube' was adopted by all guard and line infantry, dragoons, artillery and engineers in 1844. For everyday wear, a spike in the form of a grenade was worn and for parade order, a plume was fitted into the grenade. Guard units continued the previous custom of wearing a large double-headed eagle without a shield as a helmet plate. The L-G Finlandski Regiment was formed in 1818, given 'Young Guard' status in 1829 and 'Old Guard' status in 1878.

79 Army Grenadier Regiment. Officer in *surtuk*.

The *surtuk* or frock coat worn with a quilted lining proved warm, practical and popular for officers who were not at that time provided with a *shinel*. The helmet plate is of army pattern with a smaller eagle surmounting an amazon shield on which grenadier regiments had a grenade and a number.

80 Foot Artillery.
   Private in barrack order.
The helmet has a grenade spike only for everyday wear and the shield section of the helmet plate has crossed cannon superimposed with a number. The jacket is single-breasted, the pattern introduced at the beginning of Nicholas' reign for army as opposed to guard units which retained their plastrons.

Plate 31
Nicholas I, 1825–1855.
1844 Uniform Changes.

81 Volinski Lancer Regiment
   No 6. Lancer in *shinel*.
The *shinel* had become a practical and much-loved garment but was still only worn by other ranks. The lance plate is of the pattern introduced at the beginning of Nicholas' reign and lancers were little affected by the 1844 changes.

82 Life-Guard Horse Regiment.
   Officer in greatcoat.
A caped *Nicholaevski shinel* is worn over the *surtuk* and the head-dress is a *furashka*. There were by now three guard cuirassier regiments, the Cavalier Guard, L-G Horse Regiment and L-G Cuirassier His Majesty's Regiment. The fourth, the L-G Cuirassier, Her Majesty's Regiment was added in 1856.

83 Smolenski Infantry, His
   Grace the Duke of
   Wellington's Regiment.
   Soldier in winter marching
   order.
The appointment of the Duke of Wellington as Colonel was a unique honour for a British soldier and the regiment carried his name until his death in 1852. The divisional number is worn on the shoulder boards and the regimental number on the shield of the helmet plate and on the buttons.

Plate 32
Nicholas I, 1825–1855.
Caucasian Corps, 1848–1855.
The Caucasian Corps was run as an autonomous organization akin to the British India Army and new ideas were allowed more scope there than in the main army. Many of the uniform features developed by the Corps were later taken up by the army as a whole.

84 Nijegorodski Dragoon
   Regiment, 1850. Dragoon in
   parade order.
85 Nijegorodski Dragoon
   Regiment, 1850. Officer in
   parade order.
The Nijegorodski Dragoon Regiment, permanently stationed in the Caucasus, was allowed by the Tsar, who had a personal liking for the Caucasian style, to introduce Caucasian uniform of its own. After Nicholas' death, the regiment was made to conform to standard pattern dragoon uniform, but under Nicholas

II elements of this uniform were re-introduced.

86   Infantry of the Caucasian Corps. Under-officer in service order.

He wears the official issue *furashka*, *polu-kaftan* or tunic and trousers tucked into high soft boots, the whole giving a modern and practical appearance.

Plate 33
Nicholas I, 1825–1855.
Caucasian Corps, 1848–1855.

87   Grenadier Regiment H.R.H. Prince Constantine Nicholaevitch. Private in summer marching order.

The helmet has been replaced by a fur cap similar to that worn by cossacks, without badges, but with a regimental honour scroll. For the first time the *polu-kaftan* or tunic appears. He wears long white trousers for summer wear.

88   Grenadier Regiment H.R.H. Constantine Nicholaevitch. Officer in parade order.

The officer also has the fur cap and *polu-kaftan*. His *shashka*, a combination of styles with French pattern hilt and cossack blade, is worn on a belt over the right shoulder in Caucasian style with the sharp edge of the blade facing backwards.

89   Caucasian Corps Artillery. Private in marching orders.

He wears full equipment including the *tesak* or short sword. His trousers are tucked into high soft boots supported by straps just below the knee.

Plate 34
Nicholas I, 1825–1855.
Crimean War, 1853–1856.

90   Siberian Lancer Regiment No. 12. Lancer in winter marching order.

The 12th Lancers were present at the Battle of Balaclava where they nearly succeeded in cutting off the retreat of the British Light Brigade. The black oilskin covers on campaign were similar to those worn by British lancers and led to confusion between the two.

91   Ingermanlandski Hussar Regiment No. 12. Hussar in winter marching order.

Together with the Kievski Hussar Regiment No. 11 at Balaclava, they charged the 'Thin Red Line' of the 93rd Highlanders and later suffered at the hands of Scarlett's Heavy Brigade. The shako, little changed since the reign of Alexander I, was protected by an oilskin cover with the squadron number stencilled on. The cavalry sabre is the 1826 pattern based on, and in many cases converted from, the French cavalry sabre 'anne XI' pattern of which the Russians had a large number taken in 1812.

Plate 35
Nicholas I, 1825–1855.
Crimean War 1853–1856.

92   Minski Infantry Regiment. Private in winter marching order.

The Minski Regiment was part of the

1st Brigade 14th Division. The soldier wears winter dress adapted for service (compare with figure 83). His *pickelhaube* has been left in barracks and he wears his *furashka* instead. The *shinel* has its skirts gathered up and the trousers are worn tucked into boots. This regiment played an important part in the battle of the Alma.

93 Tarutinski Jaeger Regiment. Captain in winter order.

The Tarutinski Regiment was part of the 2nd Brigade, 17th Division. The officer wears a *furashka* and *shinel* of soldier's pattern. For the first time, shoulder boards or *pogoni* were worn by officers, made up from soldiers' shoulder boards with strips of officers' braid sewn on; the *polu-sabia* is worn on a belt over the right shoulder.

94 Jakutski Infantry Regiment. Private in winter marching order.

They were part of the 2nd Brigade, 11th Division and this soldier is based on a prisoner taken at the battle of the Alma. He wears the peakless *furashka* later adopted universally under Alexander III and his divisional number on the shoulder boards.

Plate 36
Nicholas I, 1825–1855.
Crimean War, 1853–1856.

95 No. 3 Don Cossack Horse Artillery Battery. Private in summer service order.

This was the battery charged in error by the British Light Brigade at Balaclava and which bravely stayed at its guns to be sabred down by the cavalry. The private wears an oilskin cover made into a separate cap for service wear, often referred to as a 'bucket'.

96 53rd Don Cossack Regiment. Cossack.

By the mid-nineteenth century, although they were still referred to as irregular cavalry, cossacks were used more and more like any other cavalry. In the Crimea they were used mainly for reconnaissance and were less effective on the occasions on which they were used in set-piece battles. Uniform had been standardized with only minor distinctions for different regions of origin.

Plate 37
Alexander II, 1855–1881.
Guard.

97 Life-Guard Preobrajenski Regiment, 1855. Private in parade order.

The white piping around plastron and cuffs of the *polu-kaftan* distinguished regiments of the 1st Guard Infantry Division, the 2nd having red and the 3rd yellow. The helmet eagle is still the Nicholas I pattern, replaced in 1857 by the new pattern with wings up. The chevrons on the sleeve denote length of service.

**98 Life-Guard Horse
Grenadier Regiment, 1855.
Subaltern officer in parade
order.**

An example of the uniform changes
originated by Nicholas I and implemented after his death by Alexander
II. The main feature of the change
was the replacement of the coatee by
a double-breasted tunic or *polu-
kaftan*, with a detachable plastron
buttoned on the front which has
remained a feature of Russian parade
uniform into modern times. The
distinctive helmet with its side-to-
side crest derived from the pattern
first introduced by Potemkin and
reintroduced by Nicholas I.

**Plate 38
Alexander II, 1855–1881.
Army Cavalry.**

**99 Life-Dragoon Pskovski,
Her Majesty's Regiment,
1860. Dragoon in parade
order, 1860.**

The uniform of dragoon regiments
was similar to that of line infantry
except for the waist sash and *shashka*
belt worn over the right shoulder.
Exclusive to this regiment are the
cypher of the Empress Maria Alexan-
drovnoa on the new pattern helmet
plate and the pink facing colour.

**100 2nd Life-Hussar
Pavlovgradski, His
Majesty's Regiment, 1855.
Field officer in parade
order.**

The *kiver* is the new 'marine pattern'
introduced in 1855 for all except
some guard regiments, which lasted

until 1862 when it was replaced by
the lower *kiver* of French style. Other
new features are the tunic-style *dolo-
man* and the loose overalls.

**Plate 39
Alexander II, 1855–1881.
Line Infantry.**

**101 Orenburgski Line
Battalion 1869. Soldier in
marching order.**

Features introduced during the reign
of Alexander II include the double-
breasted *polu-kaftan*, French-style
shapka or kepi, introduced in 1862,
and the trousers tucked into soft
boots. The black equipment denotes
a rifle regiment and the *shinel* is
worn folded around the pack.

**102 Line Infantry, 1874.
Subaltern officer in
parade order.**

The single-breasted tunic or *mundir*
replaced the *polu-kaftan* in 1872, and
in the same year, gold braid around
the *shapka* was introduced to denote
rank. The subaltern's rank is also
denoted by the epaulettes without
fringe.

**103 Life-Grenadier
Ekaterinoslavski, His
Majesty's Regiment, 1869.
Feldwebel (sergeant-
major) in summer parade
order.**

Summer order is denoted by the
white trousers. He is armed with an
officer's sword. His rank is denoted by
gold lace in shoulder boards, collar
and cuffs.

Plate 40
Alexander II, 1855–1881.
Turkestan, 1860–1881.

104 Turkestanski Line Battalion, 1870. Private in summer service order.

Army units stationed in Turkestan wore uniforms appropriate to the tropical climate including the 'Foreign Legion' style *shapka* with white cover and flap and the white linen shirt known as *gimnasticheskata rubaha*, later shortened to *gimnasterka*, worn with shoulder boards. The trousers are of buffalo-skin dyed red known by the Turkoman name *chambari*.

105 Orenburg Cossacks, 1870. Cossack.

He wears a fur hat or *papaha*, a *checkmen* or cossack style tunic with hooks in place of buttons and loose trousers with blue stripes. Armament includes a lance without pennant, a *shashka*, a pistol and lanyard and a musket worn cossack-style over the right shoulder. The pouch on the shoulder belt is for percussion caps.

106 Line Infantry, 1870. Subaltern officer in summer service order.

The wearing of the soldier's *gimnasterka* by officers was not officially approved, but they proved so comfortable on campaign that many officers adopted them. Official summer uniform for officers was the white linen *kitel*. Officer status is denoted by the gold braid *pogoni* or shoulder boards, infantry pattern sabre, the revolver in holster with black, orange and white lanyard.

Plate 41
Alexander II, 1855–1881.
Russo-Turkish War 1877–1878.

107 Don Cossacks, 1877–1878. Cossack.

The white linen *furashka* was a distinction of the Caucasian Corps and the rifle is carried in cossack style, slung over the right shoulder. The free and easy riding position is also typical of cossacks who had their own method of riding.

108 Nijegorodski Dragoon Regiment, 1877–1878. Officer.

The Nijegorodski Dragoon Regiment in line with other units of the separate Caucasian Corps, went their own way in matters of uniform. Here the officer wears his *surtuk* open over a leather *beshmet*, a circassian *kaftan*. He is armed with a regimental pattern *shashka*, a Caucasian *kinjal* (knife) and a *nagaika* (whip). He had discarded his cumbersome epaulettes.

Plate 42
Alexander II, 1855–1881.
Russo-Turkish War 1877–1878.

109 Line Infantry. Soldier in marching order.

He wears full equipment with the *shinel* rolled and carried over the left shoulder. The *shapka* has no plume and for summer wear, he has white trousers tucked into boots. At this period, the soft *shapka* was still used only by line infantry and some auxiliary units, most other units having changed back to traditional patterns of head-dress for parade order and *furashkas* for service order.

**110 Line Infantry.
Subaltern officer in greatcoat.**

The *palto* or officer's greatcoat, introduced in 1855 could be worn as a coat or as a cloak, here worn over the *mundir*, by unbuttoning the restraining belt at the back. Like the soldiers, the officer has his trousers tucked into soft boots.

**111 Line Infantry.
Drummer in summer marching order.**

The drum is of the new shallow style introduced after the Crimean War and the drummer's uniform is similar to that of ordinary rank and file with the addition of 'swallow's nest' wings.

**Plate 43
Alexander II 1855–1881.
Russo-Turkish War 1877–1878.**

**112 Army Artillery.
Private in winter marching order.**

His equipment includes the *bashlyk* or hood with long wings worn across the body or wrapped around the neck.

**113 Line Infantry.
Subaltern officer in winter marching order.**

He wears a *palto* with *bashlyk* attached

and a knapsack, indicating his subaltern rank. Armament includes a revolver and an 1841 pattern dragoon *shashka* worn in the Caucasian style.

**114 Line Infantry.
Private in summer marching order.**

The typical Russian soldier of the period, he wears the soft *shapka*, white *gimnasterka* and his *shinel* rolled and worn over his left shoulder. The change in appearance from the Russian soldier of the Crimean War twenty years earlier (Plate 35) is remarkable.

**Plate 44
Alexander II, 1855–1881.
Russo-Turkish War, 1877–1878.**

**115 Life-Guard Lancer Her Majesty's Regiment, 1877.
Gefreiter in summer campaign order.**

He wears a white *furashka* and his full dress *mundir* without plastron. The lancer element of the uniform is indicated by the cap lines and flounders worn under the *pogoni*. The chevrons on the left sleeve denote length of service.

**116 General Officer, 1877.
In *surtuk*. Grand Duke Nicholai Nicholaievitch.**

Grand Duke Nicholai Nicholaievitch was the brother of Alexander II and, against his will, was given command of the European Front during the Russo-Turkish War, a position held also by his son in 1914 (see Plate 56). He wears a white *furashka* and *surtuk* with general's *pogoni* and officer's sash. On the *pogoni* is the cypher of his father, Tsar Nicholas I. The aiguillettes indicate that he is a General-Adjutant.

117 Life-Guard Preobrajenski Regiment, 1877. Subaltern officer in summer campaign order.

Like the lancer, he wears white *furashka* and his full dress *mundir* without plastron with *pogoni* in place of epaulettes. His *shinel* is worn rolled over his left shoulder and he still wears the subaltern's knapsack. His summer-weight trousers are worn tucked into high boots and he is armed with the 1865 pattern *sablia* in metal scabbard.

Plate 45
Alexander III, 1881–1894.
Guard

118 Life-Guard Preobrajenski Regiment, 1882. Private in parade order.

Immediately upon his accession, Alexander III introduced new 'Russian style' uniforms. The soldier here wears the new pill-box shaped fur cap, referred to as *shapka* with St Andrew's star and cockade. The double-breasted tunic is fastened with hooks rather than buttons but the white piping of the 1st Guard Infantry Division has been retained.

119 Life-Guard Hussar His Majesty's Regiment, 1882. Private in service order.

Although, under Alexander III's re-forms, all army cavalry regiments were converted to dragoons, guard cavalry retained their traditional uniforms. The Life-Guard Hussar Regiment had six squadrons and was based at Tsarskoie Selo, the suburban palace near St Petersburg.

Plate 46
Alexander III, 1881–1894.
Cavalry.

120 Army Dragoon Regiment, 1882. *Wahmistr* (sergeant) in parade order.

In 1882 all line cavalry regiments were converted into Dragoons and given the new 'Russian style' uniforms which differed from infantry by the head-dress, also fur *shapkas* but cut in front to reveal the colour of the cloth and the badge. They were referred to as *dragoonskia shapka* later abbreviated to *dragoonka*. The NCOs rank was still denoted by braid on the collar and cuffs and by straps on the *pogoni*. The sleeve chevrons denoted length of service.

121 Life-Guard Dragoon Regiment, 1882. Field Officer in parade order. Grand Duke Boris Vladimirovitch.

The Life-Guard Dragoon Regiment was the only guard cavalry unit to adopt the new uniform which was similar to that of the army dragoon regiments with the St Andrew's star on the *dragoonka* in place of the eagle. The sword is the new dragoon *shashka* pattern 1881. The Grand Duke Boris

Vladimirovitch was the nephew of Alexander III.

122 Army Dragoon Regiment, 1882. *Gefreiter* (junior NCO) in parade order.

Dragoons were still expected to fight on foot as well as mounted and they carried a similar, but lighter, rifle to that used by the infantry. The pattern 1881 dragoon soldier's *shashka* had a scabbard specially designed to hold the bayonet.

Plate 47
Alexander III, 1881–1894.
Line Infantry.

Under Alexander III the line infantry comprised sixteen grenadier and 165 line regiments, each of four battalions and of four companies. A regiment had seventy officers and 1,800 soldiers.

123 Line Infantry, 1882. NCO in marching order.

He wears the standard pattern fur *shapka* with eagle and cockade for line regiments. The buttonless tunic or *mundir* fastened with hooks was supposed to give the impression that he was wearing a traditional Russian *kaftan*, part of the trend towards Russification of uniform.

124 Line Infantry, 1882. Subaltern officer in parade order.

The 1882 changes in officers' uniforms was similar to those for the rank and file. It became fashionable to wear trousers cut in the style of plus-fours. The sword is the officer's pattern 1881 *shashka*, the universal fighting sword for all officers other than those stationed in the Caucasus.

125 Line Infantry 1882. Soldier in winter order.

Apart from the fur cap, the uniform has changed little from that of the previous reign (Plate 43), including the *bashlyk* worn across the front with the wings tucked into the waistbelt.

Plate 48
Nicholas II, 1894–1917.
Russo-Japanese War 1904–1905.

The Russian army went into the Russo-Japanese war with uniforms unchanged from the time of Alexander III and the items most usually associated with the summer months of the war, the white *kitels* of the officers and *gimnasterkas* of the soldiers dated from the reforms of Alexander II.

126 Line Infantry, 1904. Subaltern officer in summer campaign dress.

As often happened on campaign, uniform regulations have been overlooked and the officer wears a soldier's *gimnasterka* with officer's *pogoni*, lanyard and sash, the last two in the 'Romanov' colours of orange, black and white.

127 General Officer, 1904. Summer campaign dress. General Kuropatkin.

General Kuropatkin wears the official white *kitel* with general's *pogoni* with the cypher of Nicholas II and aiguillettes, denoting that he is a General-Adjutant. Kuropatkin served with distinction in the Russo-Turkish War. He was war minister to Nicholas II from 1898 to 1904 when he was given command of the army in the field at the outbreak of the Russo-Japanese War. He achieved little however and was replaced in March 1905 by General Linevich.

128 Line Infantry, 1904.
       Private in summer
       campaign order.
He wears the white *gimnasterka* and peakless *furashka*. His *shinel* is worn rolled over his shoulder and his equipment includes haversack, waterbottle and ammunition pouches. The white band around his *furashka* indicates the third regiment in a division.

Plate 49
Nicholas II, 1894–1917.
Russo-Japanese War, 1904–1905.
The main weight of the war fell on the Far-Eastern Military District where in addition to regular units, local cossacks and other reserves were called out.

129 Siberian Rifles, 1904.
       Private in winter order.
Both officer and private wear the thick Siberian *papaha* (fur cap) which was distinctive to this Corps. It was worn loosely so that it could be pulled down over the ears to protect the neck. The private wears an unofficial sheepskin coat or *tulup* in place of the usual soldiers' *shinel*. This would have

been obtained from local sources but was tolerated, particularly during war-time.

130 Siberian Rifles, 1904.
       Officer in winter order.
In contrast to the soldier in figure 129, the officer wears the official issue *shinel*. His equipment includes binocular case and waterbottle and he is armed with a revolver and the pattern 1881 officer's *shashka*.

131 Don Cossacks, 1904.
       Cossack in summer
       campaign order.
By this period, the cossack was equipped similarly to, but more lightly than, ordinary regular cavalry. For example he has the shortened version of the pattern 1891 dragoon rifle and his *shashka* scabbard is not equipped to take a bayonet. He also carries a cossack *nagaika*.

Plate 50
Nicholas II, 1894–1917
Guard Infantry, service order,
1906.
Khaki was adopted for everyday wear throughout the army after the Russo-Japanese War.

132 Life-Guard Preobrajenski
       Regiment, 1906. Private in
       summer service order.
The main feature of this order of dress was the khaki *gimnasterka*. The red band around the cap denoted the first regiment in the division and the 1st Guard Infantry Division was distinguished by white piping, in this

case worn around the collar of the *gimnasterka*. Red *pogoni* were worn by all guard regiments.

133 Life-Guard Ismailovski Regiment, 1906. Subaltern officer in summer service order.

The white linen *kitel* introduced by Alexander II had been replaced by khaki. Red on the *pogoni* denotes guard, white piping around the cuff, 1st Guard Infantry Division and white band around the *furashka*, the third regiment in the division.

134 Life-Guard Litovski Regiment, 1906. *Feldwebel* (sergeant-major) in summer service order.

The L-G Litovski Regiment was part of the 3rd Guard Infantry Division, all the regiments of which wore yellow plastrons on their full dress *mundirs* and yellow piping in all orders of dress, in this case on the front of the *gimnasterka*. Again red *pogoni* denote guard status and the regiment's position as 1st Regiment in the 3rd Division is denoted by the yellow *furashka* band.

Plate 51
Nicholas II, 1894–1917.
Guard Cavalry, service order, 1906.

135 Life-Guard Hussar His Majesty's Regiment, 1906. NCO in summer service order.

He still wears the traditional red peakless *furashka* rather than the khaki version and the hussar style is also continued in the boots with bosses on the front. In other respects he is conventionally dressed in khaki *gimnasterka*. He is armed with the pattern 1881 dragoon *shashka* with fitting for bayonet on the scabbard.

136 Cavalier Guard Regiment, 1906. Officer in summer service order.

He wears the khaki *kitel* with full dress pouch-belt, sash and pistol lanyard. The white piping around the edge of the *pogoni* was a distinction of cuirassiers and the suite of the Tsar. Since he is in service order, he carries the 1881 pattern officer's *shashka* rather than the *palash* still carried by Guard Cuirassier Regiments in parade order. (See Plate 53.)

137 Life-Guard Lancer His Majesty's Regiment, 1906. Officer in summer service order.

The *kitel* is in the English style, with patch pockets, usually referred to as the 'French' after the British general. The double Sam Browne belt, adopted universally in 1913, was also taken from the British. The Lancer origin of his uniform is indicated by the full dress cap flounders tucked underneath the *pogoni*.

Plate 52
Nicholas II, 1894–1917.
Parade uniforms, 1909–1917.

With the introduction of khaki uniforms, there came a demand for more spectacular parade uniforms, particularly for guard regiments and there was a general return to the uniforms which existed before Alexander III's reforms.

138 Life-Guard Jaegerski Regiment, 1909. Colonel in parade order.

The new pattern *kiver* was introduced in 1909 for general officers, guard infantry and grenadier regiments. Guard regiments have the St Andrew's star as shako plate with regimental honour scrolls, if awarded, worn above. Guards also reverted to the double-breasted *mundir* with plastron, usually red in the 1st and 2nd Guard Infantry Divisions, but the L-G Jaegerski Regiment was allowed this special shade of green.

139 Life-Guard Hussar His Majesty's Regiment. General in parade order. Tsar Nicholas II.

The guard hussar regiments had retained their traditional uniforms even after Alexander III had converted all army hussar and lancer regiments to dragoons, and their uniform had remained virtually unchanged since the reign of Alexander II.

140 General Staff, 1909. Field officer in parade order.

As the General Staff were not part of the Guard (unless on the staff of a Guard Division), the *kiver* plate is the double-headed eagle rather than the St Andrew's star and the *mundir* has no plastron. The traditional form of epaulette had been retained, in this case indicating the rank of field officer. The aiguillette shows that the wearer is a graduate of the General Staff Academy and the collar embroidery was also distinctive to the General Staff.

Plate 53 Nicholas II, 1894–1917. Parade Uniforms, 1909–1917.

141 Life-Guard 4th Rifle Imperial Family Battalion (later Regiment), 1909. *Unteroffizier* in parade order.

The L-G Imperial Family Rifles was originally an *opolchenie* regiment, formed by Nicholas I from serfs on the crown estates around St Petersburg and their uniform was one of the first examples of the revival of the 'Russian style'. It was altered in various ways in subsequent reigns until Nicholas II restored their original dress in the 1909 changes. Their *opolchenie* origin is indicated by the *opolchenie* cross worn over the normal cockade on the *shapka*. Raspberry coloured facings were a distinction of rifle regiments.

142 Cavalier Guard, Her Majesty's Regiment, 1909. Private in dismounted palace order.

The gala and parade uniforms of the guard cuirassier division had remained virtually unchanged since the introduction of the *collet* in 1855. The red *supervest* with a large metal St Andrew's star replaced the cuirass for wear on duty inside the palace. Only the Cavalier Guard wore the St Andrew's star on the *supervest*, the L-G Horse Regiment wearing a double-headed eagle.

143   Life-Guard 1st Artillery Brigade, 1909. *Unteroffizier* in parade order.

Other ranks were issued with parade *mundirs* with plastrons and *kivers* like the officers but with less elaborate embellishments. Artillery wore black velvet collar, cuffs and plastron and their guard status is indicated also by the red shoulder boards. The L-G 1st Artillery Brigade were part of the 1st Guard Division and therefore had white piping around the cuff.

Plate 54.
Nicholas II, 1894–1917.
Parade uniforms, cavalry, 1909–1917.

In 1907–08, Nicholas II ordered that dragoon regiments which had formerly been hussars and lancers should revert to their traditional titles and that their parade uniforms should be in the traditional styles.

144   10th Lancer Odessa Regiment, 1909. Lancer in parade order.

The regimental facings of pale blue followed the arrangements which existed when they had been lancers before. All the traditional lancer features, particularly the *czapska* and plastron were revived.

145   13th Dragoon Military Order Regiment, 1909. Subaltern officer in parade order.

This regiment was often referred to as the Military Order of St George Regiment and they had the unique distinction of using the Star of St George on their appointments, in this case as a helmet plate. The regiment's previous service as cuirassiers was recognized by the adoption of a *collet* with braid down the front, in this case in black and gold to suggest the colours of the riband of the Order of St George. The Potemkin-style helmet, previously only worn by the L-G Horse Grenadier Regiment was adopted for all dragoon regiments, with a white crest for those regiments which had formerly been cuirassiers and black for the remainder.

Plate 55
Nicholas II, 1894–1917.
Parade uniforms, cossacks, 1909–1917.

146   Life-Guard Cossack His Majesty's Regiment, 1909. *Unteroffizier* in parade order.

This was the most senior of the cossack regiments. They still wore the traditional red coat, dark blue trousers and red bag on the *papaha*. A particular regimental distinction was the absence of a stripe on the trousers.

147 Life-Guard Atamanski, His Imperial Highness the Tsesarvitch's Regiment, 1913. Field officer in parade order.

The pale-blue coat, dark blue trousers with pale-blue stripe and silver lace were a distinction of this regiment. He carries a *klitch*, a romantic style of sabre which made its appearance in 1913 and was tolerated although not officially approved.

148 His Imperial Majesty's Own Convoy (Escort). Cossack in parade order.

The 'Convoy of the Tsar' was a guard unit of Caucasian cossacks formed by Nicholas I. It originally included many exotic oriental elements but Alexander III reduced it to a Kubanski *sotnia* and a Terski *sotnia*, both dressed similarly in traditional Caucasian style. The convoy formed the Tsar's own close personal escort.

Plate 56
Nicholas II, 1894–1917.
1913 uniform changes.

149 Army Artillery, 1913. Officer in parade order.

In 1913 moves were begun to abolish parade uniform for all except guard units and instead to provide parade features for the everyday khaki uniform. This officer wears the new

papaha with officer's cockade. The khaki *kitel* is worn with full dress sash, epaulettes and plastron which only partially covers the patch pockets. He carries the 1913 infantry officer's sabre worn in the European manner. Few units however received the new uniform before the outbreak of war in 1914 put an end to the reform.

150 General Officer, 1914. In summer campaign order. Grand Duke Nicholai Nicholaievitch.

He is depicted wearing a *papaha* and khaki *kitel* and trousers with general officer's stripes. Since on this occasion he was visiting the French army, he is wearing the riband and star of the Legion d'Honneur. Grand Duke Nicholai was the son of Grand Duke Nicholai Nicholaievitch who commanded the European front in the Russo-Turkish War (see Plate 44) and was nephew of Tsar Alexander II. At the outbreak of World War I he took command of the Russian armies on the European front until replaced by the Tsar himself in September 1915.

151 General Officer, 1914. In summer campaign order.

Typical of the appearance of a smart Russian officer at the outbreak of World War I, he wears a *kitel* with inset breast pockets only and a double Sam Browne. His aiguillette denotes that he is a graduate of the General Staff Academy. His *shashka* is the 1909 officer's pattern worn in the traditional Russian manner but suspended from the Sam Browne.

Plate 57
Nicholas II, 1894–1917.
World War I, 1914–1917.

**152 Line Infantry, 1914–1917.
Private in summer
campaign order.**
A typical Russian soldier of World
War I, his battered *furashka* already
shows signs of service. His khaki *gimnasterka*, his *shinel* worn rolled over his
shoulder and his khaki trousers
tucked into boots proved practical
and comfortable for active service.
The banner on his M1891 rifle is a
company marker flag.

**153 Life-Guard Preobrajenski
Regiment, 1914–1917.
Subaltern officer in
summer campaign.**
Even on campaign, there are still
signs of his guards' background in the
well tailored and pressed *gimnasterka*
and trousers. Although *gimnasterkas*
were still officially only for soldiers,
many officers wore versions of them,
in this case with pockets added. Regimental distinctions include the white
piping of the 1st Guard Infantry
Division worn around the collar of
the *gimnasterka* and the regimental
breast badge.

**154 Aviation Service, 1914–1917.
Subaltern officer in
campaign order.**
The Aviation Service was formed as
part of the Engineer Corps under
the technical guidance of the French.
He wears an engineer's *furashka* and
on his *pogoni* his aviator's emblem.
He wears a leather *tujurka*, a garment
which became increasingly popular
as the war progressed.

Plate 58
Nicholas II, 1894–1917.
World War I, 1914–1917.

**155 5th Hussar Alexandriski,
Her Imperial Majesty
The Empress Regiment,
1914. Hussar in winter
campaign order.**
A cavalry soldier in the early stages
of the war, still retaining much of his
peace-time smartness. His black
leather equipment includes waistbelt
and cartridge pouch, the short version of the M1891 pattern rifle slung
over his left shoulder and a pattern
1881 dragoon *shashka* suspended from
the sword belt over his right shoulder.

**156 Guard Artillery, 1914–1917.
Lieut.-Colonel in winter
campaign order.**
Officers were supposed to wear the
official issue soldiers' *shinel* with officers' *pogoni* and collar patches, but
they often had similar versions made
privately in better quality materials.
Over the *shinel* he wears the double
Sam Browne with a pattern 1909
officer's *shashka*.

**157 Army Infantry, 1914–1917.
Private in winter
campaign order.**
This is the uniform worn by the
majority of the ten million men that
Russia was able to put into arms during World War I. The *papaha* of
artificial wool was introduced just
before the war. The war-time economy version of the *shinel* had hooks
only and no buttons. It was usually
worn over quilted jacket and
trousers.

Plate 59
Nicholas II, 1894–1917.
World War I, 1914–1917.

158   Don Cossacks, 1914–1917.
Officer in summer
campaign order.

By 1914, cossacks were regarded in
every way as regular cavalry and
each cavalry division had one regiment each of dragoons, lancers, hussars and cossacks. Cavalry were used
extensively in the mounted role
against the Austrians but less so
against the Germans, who had dismounted their cavalry early on in the
war.

159   Automobile Unit of the
Engineer Corps. 1914–1917.
Private.

Motorized units were formed at the
outbreak of the war but were never
available in more than limited numbers. They provided staff cars and
also a few armoured car units. The
uniform retained engineer features
including *furashka* with black band
and black collar patches on the
tujurka. Drivers were in addition provided with a special emblem on the
pogoni.

Plate 60   Gorgets.

Gorgets were referred to in Russian
as *officierski znak* or officer's badge.
They were worn by dismounted
troops (infantry, foot artillery, sappers) only and were the sign of an
officer on duty.

1   Life-Guard Preobrajenski
Regiment, 1698. Gorget
worn by Tsar Peter the
Great as Colonel in Chief.

Gorgets were originally introduced
by Peter for his two guard infantry
regiments only. In 1700, after the
battle of Narva during which all the
senior officers of the two regiments
were put out of action and the regiments were led by the subalterns,
Peter granted the distinction that the
date of the action, 19 November
1700, should thereafter be inscribed
on the gorgets of the subalterns only.

2   Guard Infantry, 1731.
Gorget.

A new, more elaborate pattern of
gorget was introduced in 1731 by the
Empress Anna Iovannovna for guard
infantry and for the 1st Cadet Corps.
The Cadet Corps retained this pattern to 1917. A variety of other
patterns of gorget were introduced
during the reigns of Elizabeth and
Catherine the Great.

3   Universal Pattern, 1798.
Gorget.

The Emperor Paul introduced one
standard pattern of gorget for all regiments and for the only time, the two
senior Guard Regiments lost the distinction of wearing their battle
honours for Narva. On his assumption of the Grand Mastership of the
Maltese Order, Paul added the Maltese Cross to the double-headed eagle
on the gorget.

4   Army Infantry, 1808.
Gorget.

Alexander I simplified the design of
the gorget and reduced it in size. He
also restored the battle honours to the

gorgets of the Guard Infantry who had a more elaborate pattern.

5 Guard Infantry, 1820. Gorget.

After the Napoleonic Wars, Alexander introduced a new smaller pattern gorget which, in general style, remained unchanged until 1917. Under Alexander II the shape of the eagle was changed to 'wings up' and in 1857 they were abolished altogether for all except the two senior guard regiments and the 1st Battery, 1st Guard Artillery Brigade, which was always considered part of the L-G Preobrajenski Regiment.

6 Life-Guard Preobrajenski Regiment, 1910. Subaltern's gorget.

Nicholas II reintroduced eighteenth-century patterns of gorget for guard regiments. The date 1700 No 19, commemorating the battle of Narva was distinctive to the L-G Preobrajenski and Semenovski Regiment. For the army in general, when the parade head-dress was abolished, there was no place for honour scrolls, and regiments entitled to wear them were given gorgets with the honours inscribed.

Plate 61   Epaulettes.

Epaulettes originally appear under Catherine the Great and are occasionally found with cyphers added, but they did not have the same significance as later.

1 General Staff, 1807. General officer's epaulette.

In 1807, among the uniform changes which followed the Treaty of Tilsit and which therefore presumably owed something to French influence, Alexander introduced a system of epaulettes which remained virtually unchanged to 1917. The designs were based on three grades of rank, general officers with heavy fringes, field officers with light fringes and subaltern officers without fringes.

2 Guard Sapper Battalion, 1st Company, 1830. Field officer's epaulette.

Nicholas I introduced certain variations within the same general theme. General staff, guard infantry and cuirassiers were to have an all metal braided base as opposed to army which had a cloth base with metal braid edging. He also introduced the system of rank stars repeated later on *pogoni* (see Plate 62). The system of cyphers began to develop also. In this case, since the Tsar was Colonel-in-Chief of the unit, the 1st Company were allowed to wear his cypher.

3 Line Cavalry, 1830. Subaltern's epaulette.

Nicholas introduced metal scaled epaulettes for all cavalry except cuirassiers which continued with the metal-braided design.

4 Field Marshal, 1807–1917. Epaulette.

This is the general officer's pattern with crossed batons added to denote rank. If the Field Marshal were Colonel-in-Chief of a regiment he could also wear regimental pattern epaulettes with crossed batons added.

5 Life-Guard Cuirassier, His Majesty's Regiment, 1881–1894. Subaltern's epaulette.

The first squadron or company of every guard regiment of which the Tsar was Colonel-in-Chief was referred to as the Tsar's squadron and the Tsar's cypher was worn by all ranks on epaulettes and *pogoni*.

6 4th Finnish Rifle Regiment, 1894–1917. Colonel's epaulette.

The base cloth colour showed which Brigade the regiment belonged to, the 1st always wearing red and the 2nd blue. Until 1909, the divisional number was worn on the epaulette and *pogoni*, but it was then changed to the regimental number. If the regiment was entitled to the cypher of its Colonel-in-Chief, this was worn in place of the number.

Note: These epaulettes have been drawn in perspective as if viewed from above, thus foreshortening the fringes.

Plate 62 *Pogoni* (**shoulder boards**).

Pogoni for other ranks were first adopted on a universal basis by Alexander I as part of the uniform changes introduced at the beginning of his reign. Officer's *pogoni* were introduced during the Crimean War when it was found that epaulettes provided too conspicuous a target. As an interim measure, officers took soldiers' *pogoni* and sewed on braid from their sword belts, two pieces for subalterns and three for field officers. General officers used their broad zigzag pattern lace.

There were certain standard rules about *pogoni*. The cloth base was coloured red for guard infantry; for line infantry, the 1st Brigade had red, the 2nd blue; for Grenadiers, yellow, the 1st Grenadier Division having red piping, the 2nd blue piping, the 3rd white piping and the 4th green piping; artillery and engineers had red; general officers, convoy of the Tsar, Imperial Rifles Regiment and hussars had zig-zag pattern lace; white piping around the *pogoni* was worn by the Suite of the Tsar and by Guard Cuirassiers; cavalry wore all possible combination of lace and base colours.

1	Field Marshal	General Feldmareshal
2	General	General
3	Lieut.-General	General-Leitenant
4	Major-General	General-Maior
5	Colonel	Palkovnik
	17th Don Cossack Regiment	

6	Lieut.-Colonel	Podpolkovnik
	7th Infantry Regiment	
7	Major	Maior
	55th Artillery Brigade	
	nb. Major's rank was abolished by Alexander III in 1882	
8	Captain	Kapitan or Rotmistre
	Guard Cuirassiers	(cavalry)
9	Staff-Captain	Stabs-Kapitan or
	9th Dragoon Regiment	Stabsrotmistre (cavalry)
10	Lieutenant	Poruchik
	3rd Hussar Regiment	
11	2nd Lieutenant	Podporuchik or Cornet
	9th Grenadier Sibirski Regiment	(cavalry)
12	Ensign	Praporshik
	Army Sapper Battalion	
13	Warrant Officer	Podpraporshik
	Army Infantry (1st Brigade)	
14	Sergeant-Major	Feldwebel
	Army Infantry (2nd Brigade)	
15	Sergeant-Major	Wachtmistre (cavalry)
	Life-Guard Horse Regiment	
16	Sergeant	Starski unteroffizier
	12th Artillery Brigade	
17	Corporal	Mladchi unteroffizier
	4th Lancer Kharkovski Regiment	
18	Lance-Corporal	Gefreiter
	4th Rifle Regiment	
19	Private	Nijnichin
	1st Life-Grenadier	
	Ekaterinoslavski Regiment	
20	Officer cadet	Junker
	Tchougourski Military School	

Plate 63   Head-Dress Plates, 1807–1917.

Kiver Plates were introduced by Alexander I in 1807 when the cockade worn with the original *kiver* introduced in 1803, was supplemented by a double-headed eagle plate for guard infantry (figure 1) and by metal grenades, with three flames for grenadiers and with one for army infantry.

In 1817 a new plate (figure 2) was introduced for army infantry, dragoons, hussars, artillery and engineers based on the British Waterloo shako plate and stamped with the St Andrew's star. Guard infantry then adopted a more substantial version of the double-headed eagle (figure 3).

In 1828, Nicholas I replaced the British style plate by a double-headed eagle surmounting an amazon shield on which the regimental number, cypher or emblem were mounted (for officers) or stamped (for soldiers) (figure 4).

In 1857, Alexander II altered the state eagle emblem to the 'wings up' position and *kiver* plates were altered accordingly. As head-dress became smaller, the eagle was altered correspondingly in size but in other respects the style (figure 5) remained for parade head-dress to 1917. Guard units wore the St Andrew's star either mounted on the eagle or on its own.

The cockade originated under Peter III who issued them in the Schleswig-Holstein colours of black and orange. Alexander I added a white outer (silver for officers). The formalized stamped metal cockade, figure 6 for officers and figure 7 for soldiers was introduced for wear on the *furashka* by Nicholas I and continued in use to 1917.

Plate 64   Pouches

1   **Life-Guard Grenadier Regiment, 1742–1762.**
Officer's *podsumok* or cartridge pouch, worn on the front of the belt.

2   **Guard Horse Artillery, 1805–1855.**
Officer's *ladunka* or cartridge pouch. The standard pattern during the reigns of Alexander I and Nicholas I.

3   **Guard Cavalry, 1855–1917.**
Officer's *ladunka*.

4   **Guard Horse Artillery, 1855–1881.**
Officer's *ladunka*.

5   **Army Cavalry, 1855–1917.**
Officer's *ladunka*.

6   **13th Dragoons Military Order Regiment.**
Officer's *ladunka*. This regiment had the unique distinction of using the star of the Order of St George on its appointments.

7   **Guard Horse Artillery, 1881–1917.**
Officer's *ladunka*.

8   **Army Horse Artillery, 1881–1917.**
Officer's *ladunka*.

A List of Regiments of the Imperial Russian Army, 1914

1st Guard Infantry Division
  L-G Preobrajenski Regiment
  L-G Semenovski Regiment
  L-G Ismailovski Regiment
  L-G Jaegerski Regiment

2nd Guard Infantry Division
  L-G Moscovski Regiment
  L-G Grenadierski Regiment
  L-G Pavlovski Regiment
  L-G Finlandski Regiment

3rd Guard Infantry Division
  L-G Litovski Regiment
  L-G Keksholmski Regiment
  L-G St Petersburgski Regiment
  L-G Volynski Regiment

Guard Rifle Brigade
  L-G 1st Rifle Regiment
  L-G 2nd Rifle Regiment
  L-G 3rd Rifle Regiment
  L-G 4th Rifle Imperial Family Regiment

Guard Units not included in Divisions
  His Imperial Majesty's Own Convoy
  Company of Palace Grenadiers
  His Imperial Majesty's Own Combined Infantry Regiment
  Guard Equipage
  L-G Sapper Regiment
  Guard Feldgendarmerie Squadron

1st Guard Cavalry Division
  Cavalier Guard, Her Majesty's Regiment
  L-G Horse Regiment
  L-G Cuirassier His Majesty's Regiment
  L-G Cuirassier Her Majesty's Regiment, L-G Cossack, His
    Majesty's Regiment

L-G Atamanski His Imperial Highness the Tsarevitch's Regiment

L-G Combined Cossack Regiment

2nd Guard Cavalry Division

L-G Horse Grenadier Regiment

L-G Lancer Her Majesty's Regiment

L-G Dragoon Regiment

L-G Hussar His Majesty's Regiment

Separate Guard Cavalry Brigade

L-G Lancer His Majesty's Regiment

L-G Grodno Hussar Regiment

L-G Artillery, 1st, 2nd and 3rd Brigade, Rifle Brigade

L-G Horse Artillery, 1st to 5th Batteries, 6th Don Cossack Battery

Grenadier Regiments

1st Life-Grenadier Ekaterinoslavski Regiment

2nd Grenadier Rostovski Regiment

3rd Grenadier Pernovski Regiment

4th Grenadier Nesvijski Regiment

5th Grenadier Kievski Regiment

6th Grenadier Tavrichevski Regiment

7th Grenadier Samogitski Regiment

8th Grenadier Moskovski Regiment

9th Grenadier Sibirski Regiment

10th Grenadier Malorossiiski Regiment

11th Grenadier Phanagorski Regiment

12th Grenadier Astrakhanski Regiment

13th Life-Grenadier Erivanski Regiment

14th Grenadier Grouzinski Regiment

15th Grenadier Tifliski Regiment

16th Grenadier Mingrelski Regiment

Line Infantry

52 Divisions comprising 208 Regiments

Rifle Regiments

Siberian Rifle Regiments, 11 Divisions comprising 44 Regiments

Rifle Regiments, 5 Brigades comprising 20 Regiments

Finnish Rifle Regiments, 3 Brigades comprising 12 Regiments

Caucasian Rifle Regiments, 2 Brigades comprising 8 Regiments
Turkestan Rifle Regiments, 6 Brigades comprising 22 Regiments

Dragoon Regiments

1st Life-Dragoon Moskovski Regiment
2nd Life-Dragoon Pskovski Regiment
3rd Dragoon Novorossiski Regiment
4th Dragoon Novotroitsko-Ekaterinoslavski Regiment
5th Dragoon Kargopolski Regiment
6th Dragoon Gloukhovski Regiment
7th Dragoon Kinbourski Regiment
8th Dragoon Astrakhanski Regiment
9th Dragoon Kazanski Regiment
10th Dragoon Novgorodski Regiment
11th Dragoon Rijski Regiment
12th Dragoon Starodoubouski Regiment
13th Dragoon Military Order Regiment
14th Dragoon Malorossiski Regiment
15th Dragoon Pereiaslavski Regiment
16th Dragoon Tverski Regiment
17th Dragoon Nijigorodski Regiment
18th Dragoon Severski Regiment
19th Dragoon Arkhangelski Regiment
20th Dragoon Finlandski Regiment

Lancer Regiments

1st Lancer Petrogradski Regiment
2nd Life-Lancer Kourlandski Regiment
3rd Lancer Smolenski Regiment
4th Lancer Kharkovski Regiment
5th Lancer Litovski Regiment
6th Lancer Volynski Regiment
7th Lancer Olviopolski Regiment
8th Lancer Voznessenski Regiment
9th Lancer Bougski Regiment
10th Lancer Odesski Regiment
11th Lancer Tchougouievski Regiment
12th Lancer Belgorodski Regiment
13th Lancer Vladimirski Regiment
14th Lancer Jambourgski Regiment

15th Lancer Tatarski Regiment
16th Lancer Novoarkhangelski Regiment
17th Lancer Novomirgorodski Regiment
Daghestan Cavalry Regiment
Ossetiski Cavalry Half-Regiment
Turkomanski Cavalry Half-Regiment

Hussar Regiments
1st Hussar Soumski Regiment
2nd Life-Hussar Pavlovgradski Regiment
3rd Hussar Elizabethgradski Regiment
4th Hussar Marioupolski Regiment
5th Hussar Alexandriski Regiment
6th Hussar Kliastitski Regiment
7th Hussar Belorousski Regiment
8th Hussar Loubenski Regiment
9th Hussar Kievski Regiment
10th Hussar Ingermanlandski Regiment
11th Hussar Izioumski Regiment
12th Hussar Ahtyrski Regiment
13th Hussar Narvski Regiment
14th Hussar Mitavski Regiment
15th Hussar Ukrainski Regiment
16th Hussar Irkoutski Regiment
17th Hussar Tchernigovski Regiment
18th Hussar Nejinski Regiment

Army Artillery Brigades

Army Horse Artillery Brigades

Army Sapper Battalions

Army Pontoon Battalions

Army Railway Battalions

Army Transport Battalions

Army Intendance Companies and Depots

Cossacks
Don Cossacks, Orenburg Cossacks, Astrakhan Cossacks, Uralski Cossacks, Siberski Cossacks, Semiretchski Cossacks, Transbaikalski Cossacks, Amourski Cossacks, Oussourski Cossacks, Kubanski Cossacks and Terekski Cossacks

Glossary

General military terms

Armia	Army, used mainly to denote line regiments from guard
Dragoonski	Dragoons
Gvardia	Guard
Opolchenie	Territorial army
Pehota	Infantry
Polk	Regiment
Rota	Company
Vsvod	Platoon
Voisko	Army

Pre-Petrovian military terms

Dvoriani	Yeomanry militia
Golova	Officer (literally 'head')
Innozemni	Foreign mercenary regiments
Poteshni	'Playmates', the children's regiments of Peter the Great
Pushkari	Artillery
Soldatski	Modernized regiments of Peter the Great which gradually replaced *dvoriani* and *strelzi*
Strelzi	'Shooter', the professional military caste of the sixteenth and seventeenth centuries
Voyevoda	Leaders of troops

Ranks. See description of Plate 62.

Uniform terms
Head-dress (golovni ubor)

Bashlik	Hood
Dragoonka	Dragoon cap introduced under Alexander III when all army cavalry were converted to dragoons, shortened from '*dragoonskia shapka*'

Furashka	Forage cap
Grenadierka	Grenadier cap
Kaska	Helmet
Kiver	Shako
Kubanka	Fur cap of Kuban style
Papaha	Fur cap
Shapka	Cap or hat, from Polish *Czapska*
Shliapa	Hat, also from Polish *Czapska*
Treugolka	Tricorne

Over-wear

Burka	Caucasian cloak of goat fur or felt, usually stiff, with square shoulders
Chekmen	Cossack version of *surtuk* (qv) fastened with hooks instead of buttons
Cherkeska	Cossack coat of Circassian style with cartridge pockets sewn on chest
Kaftan	Coat
Mentik	Hussar pelisse
Palto	Officer's greatcoat as issued in 1855
Shinel	Soldier's greatcoat
Surtuk	Frock coat (from French 'surtout')

Upper-wear

Collet	Cuirassier jacket with hooks in place of buttons
Doloman	Hussar jacket
Gimnasterka	Shirt, shortened version of *gimnasticherkaya rubaha* (gymnastic shirt)
Kitel	Tunic, originally white for summer wear, later khaki
Kurtka	Short jacket
Mundir	Uniform jacket
Polu-kaftan	Tunic, literally 'half-kaftan'
Tujurka	Casual jacket for everyday wear in modern times, generally leather

Accoutrements

Epauleti	Epaulettes
Kushak	Soldier's girdle
Pogoni	Shoulder boards

Kokada	Cockade
Liadunka	Pouch
Patronna sumka	Cartridge pouch
Patrontache	Cossack cartridge pouch
Pribor	Uniform ensemble or furniture, generally used to denote colour of appointments and lace (i.e. usually gold or silver)
Ranetz	Knapsack
Sharf	Sash
Shnur	Hussar's shoulder cord
Tashka	Sabretache
Veshovi meshok	Haversack
Znak	Insignia, badge

Lower Wear

Lampasi	Stripe on trousers
Bruki	Breeches
Chakchiri	Hussar breeches worn with boots
Pantaloni	Pantaloons, trousers
Shtany	Trousers
Chembari	Buffalo hide trousers dyed red, used by Turkoman troops
Botforti	Cuirassier boots
Sapogi	Boots

Weapons, edged and polearms

Baginet	Plug bayonet
Esponton	Spontoon
Kinjal	Cossack dagger
Klitch	Asiatic pattern sabre
Pallash	Straight heavy cavalry sword
Pika	Lance
Polu-sabli	Half-sabre, hanger or short infantry sword
Sabla	Sabre
Shashka	Caucasian pattern sword
Shpaga	Small sword, epée
Shtyk	Bayonet
Temliak	Sword knot

Tesak	Short sword for sappers, etc

Weapons, firearms

Automaticheski pistolet	Automatic pistol
Carabin	Carbine
Pistolet	Pistolet
Pulemet	Machine-gun
Revolver	Revolver
Rujio	Musket
Vintovka	Rifle

Bibliography

J. S. Curtiss, *The Russian Army Under Nicholas I, 1825–1855*, Durham, N.C., Duke University Press, 1965.

F. De Jongh, *L'Armée Russe*, Paris, Lemercier, 1895.

R. Furneaux, *The Siege of Plevna*, London, Anthony Blond, 1958.

M. Gayda and A. Krijitsky, *L'Armée Russe sous le Tsar Alexandre Ier de 1805 à 1815*, Paris, Le Sabretache, 1955.

F. V. Greene, *Sketches of Army Life in Russia*, London, W. H. Allen, 1881.

A. Mollo, *Army Uniforms of World War I*, Poole, Blandford Press, 1977.

* E. Mollo, *Russian Officers' Gorgets*, from *Passée Militaire*, Nos 70, 74, Paris, 1964–5.

E. Mollo, *Russian Military Swords 1801–1917*, London, Historical Research Unit, 1969.

J. Mollo, *Military Fashion*, London, Barrie and Jenkins, 1972.

J. Mollo, *Uniforms of the Seven Years War 1756–1763*, Poole, Blandford Press, 1977.

* A. V. Pomarnaski, *Portraits of A. V. Souvorov*, Leningrad, 1963.

* Colonel Saionchkovski, *Defence of Sevastopol and the Deeds of its Defenders*, St Petersburg, 1899.

* P. A. Saionchkovski, *Autocracy and the Russian Army on the border of the 19th and 20th Centuries*, Moscow, 1973.

A. Seaton, *The Crimean War, A Russian Chronicle*, London, Batsford, 1977.

* V. K. Shenk (Ed.), *Dragoon Regiments to 15 July 1897*, St Petersburg, 1898.

* V. K. Shenk (Ed.), *Grenadier and Infantry Regiments to 1 Apr 1898*, St Petersburg, 1898.

* V. K. Shenk (Ed.), *Imperial Guard to 1 May 1910*, St Petersburg, 1910.

* V. K. Shenk (Ed.), *Rules for the Wearing of Uniform by officers ...*, St Petersburg, 1910.

* V. K. Shenk (Ed.), *Tables of Uniforms of the Russian Army to 1 Apr 1911*, St Petersburg, 1911.

N. Stone, *The Eastern Front 1914–1917*, London, Hodder and Stoughton, 1975.

* I. D. Sytin (Ed.), *Military Encyclopaedia* (A to P only), 18 vols, St Petersburg, 1911–15.

* A. V. Viskovatov, *Historical Description of the Uniforms and Armaments of the Russian Army*, 30 vols, St Petersburg, 1844–56.

V. V. Zvegintsov, *The Russian Army 1914*, Paris, 1959.

* Russian titles have been translated into English.